D0856636

Parenting Your Aging Parents

by

Francine Moskowitz

and

Robert Moskowitz

Key Publications
Woodland Hills, California

Cataloging Data
Moskowitz, Francine and Robert

Parenting Your Aging Parents
Includes bibliographic references. Includes Index.
ISBN: 0-9624415-0-3; $19.95
1. Parents, Aged — Care — United States. 2. Adult
children — United States — Family relationships. 3.
Caregivers — United States — Psychology. 4. Aged —
Services for — United States. 5. Middle Age — United
States — Family Relationships. 6. Old Age Assistance —
United States. 7. Aged — Psychology. I. Moskowitz,
Francine and Robert. II. Title.
HQ1064U5M 1991
362.6M   90-92272

Library of Congress Catalog Card Number: 90-92272
ISBN: 0-9624415-0-3
© Copyright 1991
by Francine Moskowitz and Robert Moskowitz

All Rights Reserved. No part of this work may be reproduced
or transmitted in any form by any means, electronic or
mechanical, including photocopying or recording, or by any information storage or retrieval system, except as explicitly per-
mitted in writing by the Publisher. To request such
permissions, or to communicate with the authors, write to:
Key Publications, P.O. Box 6375, Woodland Hills, CA 91365.

Manufactured in the United States of America.
First Printing: January, 1991
10 9 8 7 6 5 4 3 2 1

DEDICATION

This book is dedicated to our parents:

Samuel Levy, who died at the age of 83 on May 25,
    1990, after a long and slow decline;
Ruth Levy, who did everything she could to make his
    last years peaceful;
George Moskowitz, who survived three devastating
    heart attacks and still managed to live long past
    the birth of his first great-granddaughter;
Carolyn Moskowitz, who instinctively devoted her
    own declining capabilities to preserving and
    protecting her husband;
and to everyone who ever loved or knew these people
    and suffered with them;
and to anyone everywhere who helps an aging parent
    live a little better, or longer, or happier.

With Special Thanks To:

Victoria Branch
Jack Getz
Phil Hopkins
Myra Margolis Katz, P.A.-C.
Ira L. Mintz, M.D.
Alex Moskowitz
Jake Moskowitz
Roann Rubin
Roberta Suber, M.S.W.
Deborah Weiss, M.P.H.

Preface

Aging Vikings in the year 500 A.D. presented no problems to their grown children. When they became too aged and weak to fend for themselves — usually at just forty or fifty years of age — their family would set them adrift in a favorite boat, never to be seen again. Their care and quality of life was left very directly and permanently to fate.

Today, it sounds absurd to suggest you would leave the welfare of your aging parents to fate. But if you make no better plan to care for them, that is precisely what you do.

The fact is, your parents are getting older — and probably weaker — every day. As time goes by, they are likely to require more and more assistance to maintain a lifestyle that doesn't tie your stomach in knots. Failure to plan and to act in your parents' best interests does not eliminate the problem. It simply gives other factors, usually random ones, much greater control over your aging parents' health, safety and lifestyle.

The saying: "If you fail to plan, you're planning to fail" applies with a vengeance to your responsibilities toward aging parents. No matter how you feel right now, you will almost certainly suffer some pain and anxiety tomorrow if you make too small an effort on their behalf today.

Table of Contents

Introduction

There's a simple reason we did the research and interviewing, and wrote this book: We needed the information, and we couldn't find it on any bookshelf in the country. As we went through the experience of caring for our own aging parents, we had to face the tedious, difficult and painstaking task of searching out all the relevant information we needed to understand their problems, define their options and opportunities, and help them formulate the best possible responses and decisions.

We had to deal with problems of housing, government and private health insurance, financial affairs, physical deterioration and medical care, legal matters, emotional considerations, family issues and ultimately death. We had to cope with uncomfortable issues, and make decisions that would help our aging parents without throwing the family into emotional chaos or financial hardship.

We were surprised to discover how hard it was to find out about our parents' problems and what we could do to help. We didn't expect this to be so difficult, particularly since Francine has been helping to manage hospitals and medical enterprises for almost twenty years. But the problems were very complex with many subtleties, and there were so many obstacles to understanding our parents' situation that we were very nearly overwhelmed. We eventually woke up to the idea that others might need some assistance in obtaining and understanding the same type of information. They would almost certainly need some support in choosing what to do for their parents, and when to do it.

We were right. Over the years we've been caring for our own parents, we've been continually amazed at the sheer number of families afraid to face the reality of their parents' growing weakness, or struggling to cope with the same sort of problems that still confront us. As with raising children, caring for aging parents is different in every family. But everyone faces similar issues, emotions and demands. What's most surprising — given the vast number of Americans presently in this fix — is the scarcity of information about how best to help and deal with parents (or other relatives) as they become infirm and dependent due to age. We encountered a completely fragmented system which demanded our perseverance and utmost efforts before yielding the needed information and services for our aging parents.

This will have to change in the very near future. Why? Because almost all of us are going to have to deal with problems of aging family members. There are presently more than thirty-one million Americans over the age of 65, and the number is growing at nearly twice the rate of the general population. Americans over 85 form the fastest growing population group in this country, and those over 75 form the next fastest growing group. Already, more than seven million older Americans suffer from chronic conditions requiring long term care, generally by family members. Inevitably, that number will grow, if only because medical science has fought successfully against many acute diseases, but hasn't banished them. Increasingly, medical science has commuted death sentences to sentences of longer life with chronic problems. According to a study recently prepared by the U.S. Congress, half of all Americans over age 85 (and a quarter of those over 65) cannot survive a week without receiving some form of help from others. Some of this help comes from public and private social service agencies. Most of it comes from their families. Most often, we have to care for our parents and in-laws. But many of us will wind up caring for spouses, step-parents, aunts, uncles, brothers, or sisters as well.

In surveys by major employers, between one-third and one-half of working Americans report they care for their parents or older relatives as many as thirty-five hours per week. A recent survey by the Department of Health and Human Services found that half of all working Americans care for dependent relatives, and that nearly three quarters of these caregivers occasionally stay home from work to do so. According to a recent study by the Older Women's League, nearly one third of women in America simultaneously care for young children and aging parents. In fact, it now appears common for a woman to spend at least as many years caring for her aging parents as for her own children. In addition, for every three hours of parent care women provide, men provide at least another hour.

Although the demand for parent care is already immense, it's likely to grow larger before it grows smaller. The United Way of America's Strategic Institute recently projected that the proportion of Americans aged 35 to 54 will continue to increase in future decades, as it has in the past two decades. By comparison, the proportion of Americans over age 75 will skyrocket during the same period. The World Future Society predicts this "graying of America" will create a wave of culture shock, inter-generational conflict and major changes in our society.

The result: millions of Americans are going to become part of extended families having more parents than children needing care. Very soon, they — and you — will face the emotional and practical dilemmas that come with caring for an aging relative. Fortunately, parenting your aging parents does not require all your time, effort, and concern. You can bring great improvements to your parents' quality of life with fairly simple, easy and inexpensive efforts, particularly if you face up to the need for caregiving when it first arises.

Families are working hard to care for their aging parents, yet society is able to meet only a small part of the tremendous need for aging parent care. One reason is the relative scarcity of organized support services. In this land of free enterprise, society takes a largely "laissez-faire" approach to caring for parents who need daily assistance. Literally thousands of people with their own ideas about how to meet the needs of the elderly have launched their own unique programs. They have set up services without a national, regional, or local plan to guide them. Few government agencies or private organizations have set standards for diagnosis, treatment, or terminology.

The situation is rapidly approaching chaos. All over America, a variety of imaginative and useful services do exist for the elderly. But you can't always find the ones you need in your town — or gain access once you find them. Except through word-of-mouth, it's difficult for families to locate vital services. Even when located, most of the good ones are so crowded or restricted there's little chance to get your own parents enrolled in the program.

Survey after survey shows too many families have a hard time obtaining even basic medical care for aging parents. More than half of all families seeking social and other support services for their aging parents find it a difficult process. It's even more of a problem when the family budget rules out certain options.

Because caring for aging parents is not the most pleasant subject for casual conversation, most people don't learn much from their friends and acquaintances. (Although with the "graying of America," it won't be long before the hot topics of cocktail party conversations shift from imported cars and consumer electronics to nursing homes and Medicaid benefits.) Middle-aged men and women rarely anticipate how their lives will be affected by having to take responsibility for their aging parents. Nor do they formulate plans for handling these responsibilities. Families often receive strong warnings — but don't recognize approaching problems or take action to avoid them until they suddenly discover how much deterioration has taken place since the last visit. The common pattern is to wait until a family crisis actually hits, then ask friends and acquaintances for advice. This might work with a plumbing problem or a broken TV. But each family is different; the solution that worked for your friends' or neighbors' aging parents may not work at all for you.

As your parents age, you'll be under pressure to find the best response to each new emotional bombshell that arises. First, you'll first want to rely on professionals who can diagnose any medical and psychological abnormalities. You may also want to consult lawyers and others who can help you make the necessary arrangements for the best possible caregiving. Later, you'll want to investigate a broader range of resources and assistance, and better develop your own ways of helping your parents by selecting bits and pieces from the success stories of other families.

Giving your parents this kind of parenting need not be solely a drain of time and energy. The process of caring for older family members can easily become a source of deep satisfaction. It can bring the family closer together. Any family member can gain a strong, lasting pleasure from fulfilling these important responsibilities, including young children who have the opportunity to help Grandma and Grandpa.

All this is true whether your family includes two aging couples, or only a single, widowed parent. It's true whether the adult children who find themselves parenting their aging parents have strong marriages with precisely two children, or whether they live as single parents or some other way. Your family may include combinations of divorced, remarried or otherwise re-partnered parents now in their advanced years. Rather than parents, the people requiring care may be your in-laws, your spouse, aging step-parents, aunts or uncles or cousins. Instead of their adult children, the caregivers may be nieces or nephews, or grandchildren.

For convenience, we use phrases like "aging parents" for those needing help and "adult children" for those providing it. For variety and grammatical accuracy, we sometimes mention a single "parent" and other times both "parents." Don't be misled or confused. The same considerations apply no matter who or how many you are helping, and no matter what family relationships are involved.

We structured this book so you can easily find the information you need, using either the Table of Contents or the Index. You may want to turn directly to the pages you need, but we hope you'll read the book cover to cover when you get the chance because we provide a lot of valuable information, experience and advice throughout. To help present the information more clearly, we tell stories about several "composite" families. These anecdotes and illustrative examples are based on true family experiences, but are altered and combined to help convey some important points more vividly.

All in all, the concepts, formulas, and decision-making processes presented in this book will help you anticipate as well as cope with problems you will encounter. In fact, the information in this book is important to everyone, in every walk of life. Wealthy families will need it, though they may be able to hire all the help required to maintain their parents in a comfortable lifestyle. Money will not buy freedom from the responsibilities or emotional burdens of caring for parents who no longer can care for themselves.

Low-income families will also need this book — despite having fewer options than families with greater financial resources. The information and advice in these pages will help anyone make the most of the options they *do* have. It will greatly aid any effort to prevent family members debilitated by age from sliding into an uncomfortable and unsatisfying lifestyle.

The great majority of middle-income families also need the information in this book. Their range of options and resources leaves them with agonizing choices and significant risk of losing what they already have. They usually don't have enough money to solve every one of their aging parents' problems in the easiest, most satisfying way. But they can still make a significant difference in their parents' quality of life by making the most of whatever options and opportunities they can provide.

We've received countless letters and phone calls from families we've contacted that confirm the ideas, principles and concrete information in this book. We wish you and your family the best of luck, and we hope you'll tell us of your own experiences by writing to the publisher's address in the front of this book.

— Francine and Robert Moskowitz

CHAPTER 1

ISSUES OF RESPONSIBILITY

Who Should Take Responsibility?

Take a good, hard look at your parents.

One day Dad is vigorous and excited about life. He's avidly pursuing his latest interest — perhaps gardening, investments, Little League, walking, or reading. But then a stroke, a fall, a heart attack, or a sudden illness lays him low, and he's very slow to recover. Or it may happen more gradually, as a chronic condition begins to get worse. Whatever the pattern, there will come a day when you recognize him for the frail human being he has become.

The same thing can happen to Mom. For years, she's been busy, happy, eagerly anticipating her next vacation or a chance to spend time with the grandchildren. But then Dad's health problems send her reeling into a deep depression. Or she suffers her own fall or severe illness. Perhaps a chronic condition flares up worse then ever, or sudden family difficulties overwhelm her. One day, she's no longer her former self, and she needs someone to give her daily care.

Just as upsetting is the mental deterioration caused by Alzheimer's Disease, strokes, medical conditions, or other problems associated with aging. Although the body can remain strong, the mind — and the personality — can fade so far that the parent you once knew essentially disappears forever. Whether it happens quickly or slowly, mental deterioration can create as much or more family sorrow than other problems of aging.

When either one of your aging parents takes to bed — whether in the hospital or at home — everyone in the family feels the pain and pays some of the price. Over the years — particularly the years when your parents are feeling their advancing ages — these episodes inevitably take a significant toll. The young man and woman who once hoisted you on their shoulders and solved all of your daily problems have now aged. They don't bounce back from the inevitable problems of life as well as they once did. They're not as vigorous, not as strong, nowhere near as capable of living independently as they once were.

Much of the time, of course, your parents don't need your help. They may take longer to get where they are going, or drop a few more dishes as they clean up from dinner. But they may remain capable of living independently until quite an old age. However, at any moment the situation can change. Your parents' capacities can diminish rapidly, and begin to compromise their quality of life or personal safety. If your parent is widowed or divorced and living alone, an otherwise minor illness or accident can quickly decrease their independence, perhaps permanently. A simple fall that injures an elbow or an arm, for instance, can lead to a downward spiral that's difficult to stop. At a certain point, it's time for someone in the family to step up to the responsibility and take reasonable actions to help them. The question is not whether they need help, but when, how much, and who will provide it.

Some family members will volunteer to help sooner than others, but almost everyone eventually wants to do something to help their parents. Nevertheless, distraught families with unresolved problems provide ample evidence that just wanting to help is not enough. You have to take action, change your behavior and possibly inconvenience yourself. Fortunately, it's well within your power to make a difference. Once you take the time to understand the situation and the resources available, you almost certainly can make significant improvements to your parents' quality of life.

Can Your Parents Take Full Responsibility?

The most obvious choice for the people to be primarily responsible for your parents' quality of life is simple: your parents should do everything they possibly can for themselves. One of the best ways you can help is to give them plenty of verbal reassurance and emotional support. When aging starts to weaken or slow them down, your words and deeds can help them remain confident and, to the extent possible, in charge of their own lives.

The Warmont family, from a small Midwestern town, had a strong tradition of supporting each other's best efforts. Martha and John had rarely criticized their four children's activities when they were growing up. As Brent, Samantha, Priscilla and John, Jr. each married and started their own families, they treated their parents the same way. Now well past 80, Martha and John Warmont have moved to a small apartment. In addition to their arthritis and blood pressure problems, they're noticing losses in eyesight, endurance and mental alertness.

Nevertheless, they strive to do their own shopping, cooking and cleaning. John has given up duck hunting, carpentry and auto maintenance, but still drives the family car. Martha rarely bakes her own bread or cakes any more, but still has friends over to play cards once a week.

Although Martha and John have slowed down in recent years, the aging couple feels no shame or depression over their diminished capabilities. Their adult children help and offer advice when asked, of course. But they also encourage their parents to maintain as much of their former active and independent lifestyles as they can. They let their parents cope with life's normal problems and challenges in their own way, at their own pace. Without the emotional support from their adult children, the Warmonts might have decided they were incapable of living independently, and might have become much more of a burden on their family.

We see it in family after family. Strong encouragement and emotional support help parents who are feeling vulnerable avoid becoming discouraged and disheartened. They don't fall into the trap of resenting their inability to do the same work they once did, to shoulder the same burdens, or to handle the same responsibilities. They are much more likely to sidestep depression — one of the first and most classic reactions to the slowly dawning recognition of their advancing age and diminished capabilities.

In contrast, aging parents who don't get strong family support often suffer emotional collapse and allow themselves to become depressed or overly dependent on others. This is particularly common when overly-solicitous adult children mistakenly believe "doing" for their parents is the same as "caring" for them.

Clearly, it's not emotionally healthy to "baby" your parents for too long. They're likely to resent it. Your parents are not children, no matter how child-like they may eventually become. They deserve the dignity and the self-esteem they will derive from taking care of themselves to the best of their abilities. Keep your parents as independent as possible — consistent with a healthy and satisfactory quality of life — until and unless their reduced capacities actually jeopardize their safety and well-being.

If you take too much responsibility for controlling your parents' living conditions and lifestyle, you may be asking for long-term trouble. You can become angry and resentful over what *they* are doing to *you*. You may come to dislike every one of your parents' individual weaknesses and intrusions. From there, the relationship usually deteriorates. Your parents will probably notice your anger, and will feel guilty, confused and angry in return. To compensate, they'll usually do something that makes you even angrier, continuing the cycle. By trying to do too much for your parents, you're most likely to create a "no win" scenario that can leave everyone in the family wishing for an end — any end — to the situation.

You and the rest of your family can help your parents as they grow older without having this destructive pattern take hold. The rule of thumb is: *Maintain a very optimistic attitude*. Presume your parents' growing feelings of depression and anxiety are only temporary. Recognize these feelings as parts of the *aging* syndrome, with peaks and valleys, and make strong efforts to avoid treating your aging parents unnecessarily like dependent children.

It's much more fruitful to behave as though your parents will be back on their feet in a short time. In a surprising number of cases, they will. Even if your parents never recover their full vigor, they will appreciate and benefit from your continuing faith in their abilities and strive to fulfill your expectations. Your positive and optimistic attitude will also short circuit some needless worry and conflict within the family.

However, since millions of aging parents *will* need direct intervention and help, it remains important to ask: "Who should take responsibility when your parents can no longer handle it themselves?"

Can Another Family Member Take Over?

In many families, one sister or brother is far better suited than another to take primary responsibility. A number of considerations can make this so: living closer to parents, having older children who need less care, having more money or more free time, or having special knowledge — perhaps concerning social services or health care issues, legal requirements, or financial dealings — that better suits them for dealing with the problems and opportunities of parenting aging parents.

Most of us are quite ready for someone else to step forward and help our aging parents because we fear that caregiving can be a major burden. We feel so overcommitted with family, work and daily responsibilities that we have little time or energy to spare for yet another obligation.

If you truly feel a particular brother or sister, niece or nephew would be the best caregiver, don't automatically assign them that responsibility. They may face hidden complications that would make caring for your parents too burdensome. Each person must accept responsibility freely. When you use pressure, guilt, or other family manipulations to force someone else to accept responsibility, it just makes matters worse. They can feel resentful and unhappy, and may take out their feelings on the very ones they are supposed to help.

For example, the Carson family went through a major battle over who would care for Frank and Margaret, their aging parents. Larry, the oldest son, led the rest of the family in convincing Katherine, who lived closest to their parents, to take primary responsibility. Although she tried her best, Katherine was not well suited to help her domineering father make decisions. She wept every time she saw her mother in the wheelchair. After a few months, Katherine's own children began to resent the time their mother spent with their grandparents. Katherine had frequent fights with her husband over the time she spent visiting her mother in the nursing home. For these and various other reasons, Katherine missed important opportunities to have medical problems diagnosed as early as possible, and to protect her parents' finances.

Her brother and the rest of the family began to feel Katherine was intentionally doing a bad job and hurting their parents. Katherine naturally felt pressured and judged. After their parents died, the adult children stopped talking to each other. That was five years ago, and the family is still torn apart.

Can Your Aunts and Uncles Help Out?

Aging parents Joe and Millie Ginsberg want to absolve their adult children of any caregiving responsibilities by having their own brothers and sisters look after them. From their point of view, there are advantages.

Joe trusts his younger brother Bill to make sure all the bills are paid and to invest his money conservatively. Millie is happy to see her sisters every day or two, and is less embarrassed to discuss her bladder and bowel problems with them than with her children.

This is fairly common. Many parents never become comfortable discussing very personal matters with their own children. They will often feel more at ease revealing their age-related infirmities to their brothers and sisters, with whom they established close and protective relationships long ago. When one brother or sister becomes incapacitated, he or she may feel more comfortable relying on these well-established relationships for help and emotional support than going to their own adult children.

Clearly, brothers and sisters are the number one choice to take caregiving responsibility when an aging person has no spouse or children. Very often, this is how nieces and nephews get involved: parents begin caring for an aging brother or sister, and when the effort becomes too much, hand down the responsibility to their own children.

Caregiving by siblings, however, has some inherent weaknesses. For example, Millie and Joe Ginsberg's brothers and sisters are close to their age. Far less vigorous than they used to be, Bill, Golda, Rose and Ceil may soon need help of their own. Although the Ginsberg family is still in good health and has adequate financial resources, in many families an aging parent's brothers and sisters need more help than they can give, and may not be able to sustain their caregiving effort for very long.

Moreover, aging uncles and aunts — much as they want to help — may be severely limited in what they can do for your parents. They often lack the qualifications, personal and financial resources, professional contacts and possibly the understanding of caregiving options and limitations.

Can You Rely on The Government?

When no one in the family steps forward to shoulder the responsibility for aging people, a local, regional, or state agency will generally provide minimal care in public institutions. If there is no family member that can, or will, provide help, the state will ask a court to grant it permanent authority to care for the aging person. As part of the process, the state will normally take all of that person's assets and apply them toward the cost of care in a publicly funded facility.

But this rarely happens. In most families, the state never has to take full legal responsibility. States usually exhaust every effort to find someone in the family to take charge. State agencies expect a family member to make most of the decisions and pay for most of the services the aging parents require. Some public services are free, but nearly all of the states are now moving toward a "cost sharing" approach to services for the elderly, particularly expensive services such as homemaking and senior adult day centers. Naturally, the family can use publicly funded programs and facilities in the mix of personal and institutional care they arrange.

This works out well, because local, state, and federal agencies concerned with the elderly offer a wide range of services. The most common sources of assistance include the Veterans Administration, Social Security and county or local social service departments. There are also hundreds of other government agencies and publicly funded organizations providing services to the elderly. [See the Resource Guide for a partial listing of helpful organizations and agencies.]

Depending on your parents' or your family's financial situation, local, state, or federal agencies can provide perfectly acceptable services free or at relatively low cost. While many families depend heavily on government services to maintain a good quality of life for aging parents, few can obtain from government agencies all the help they need. Nor is there any "one stop shopping." Each agency operates in its own location, under its own rules, and with its own priorities. Most likely, you'll need to pick and choose a combination of services from a variety of sources.

The type, quality and extent of government services also tend to be political footballs; they are subject to budget restrictions and sudden elimination, as well as restrictive or politically-motivated eligibility. Poverty standards, for example, are almost never set at a fair assessment of what it costs a family to live, but at an artificial level designed to keep program costs at politically and economically acceptable levels. Also, all these factors can change completely with each new wave of government officials.

What's more, even the best government agencies tend to perform slowly, and can be unresponsive. Expect long lines and longer waiting lists when you go for government help. Expect to be pigeon-holed rather than treated as an individual. Some people purposely avoid government social service agencies because they can be so bureaucratic and frustrating.

Despite all these problems, millions still arrive at middle age naively trusting that local, county, state and federal government agencies will automatically provide important social services as they need them. If you believe this, you're dead wrong, and you'll likely be in for a rude awakening.

As a practical matter, most government-sponsored social service agencies gear their programs to support a distinctly lower quality of life than many aging Americans can maintain for themselves, particularly when families provide some help. In addition, sliding scale fees for services are geared to help only relatively poor families. As with Medicaid, many government agencies require aging clients to be placed in a nursing home before they can receive certain important benefits — even when that placement is otherwise unnecessary. Government-funded services can also require clients to spend themselves into poverty before becoming eligible for benefits.

In the Tidwell family, for example, Mary and Bart managed to reach their late seventies with a comfortable nest egg. Then Bart suffered a massive stroke and began to deteriorate. Within six months he was confined to a nursing home. The state would not pay for any of his care until sixteen months later, when Bart finally qualified for aid because Mary had used up much of their savings, and had sold their home and car.

The laws that govern such situations are improving, however. Some newer state laws now allow aging citizens to retain their homes. States can still require families to deplete their other assets before granting aid for long-term care, but present federal guidelines allow the spouse of a Medicaid recipient to have a net worth as high as $62,500, plus the family home. Nevertheless, some financial dangers still remain. Many states are now making claims against the estates of those served at public expense. They see this as a way to recoup some or all of the cost of benefits previously provided.

Aside from the eligibility and repayment issues, another reason government agencies might not be the best place for your parents to find help is that they generally place a strong emphasis on physical health services. This is appropriate for some families, but *your* parents may have a greater need for socially- and emotionally-oriented support programs instead.

For example, Gilbert and Alisha Thompson had little luck getting help for their aging parents from social service agencies in their Southern state. Carl and Joanne Thompson, both nearing 80, had no serious disabilities and were given a clean bill of health by local physicians. Although they were weak and tired most of the time and could no longer drive, they failed to qualify for the help they needed most — transportation services, stimulating hobby and education programs, cleaning and maintenance services for their large home, and the like. They became isolated and bored in the rambling structure, and began feeling helpless. They had no desirable options until Gilbert and Alisha began to help them get out and around, and hired a private aide to help care for them.

Securing government help for your parents may also be complicated if they feel uncomfortable receiving public assistance. For many older people, help from the government carries the stigma of poverty and dependence. They can perceive an assistance check, a free meal delivered to their home, a van ride or the use of a room for Bingo games as "charity." To parents who have been fiercely independent all their lives, suddenly taking such "charity" can do major damage to feelings of self-worth.

There's no easy remedy for this problem. Many people, particularly older ones, won't easily change their ideas of what constitutes charity or dependence. You may want to encourage your parents to be more open-minded about accepting beneficial services. Mary and Bart Tidwell had problems accepting "charity," but were always willing to accept their Social Security checks. Most people feel the same, because they think of this as money they earned throughout their working lives. You may be able to help your parents accept other public aid — which is also funded by taxes — as other forms of assistance they've already earned.

A different problem arises when your parents will accept "welfare," but object to the kinds of people with whom they must associate in these public programs. Your parents may not want to spend time with certain ethnic groups, handicapped or disabled people, or perhaps anyone who seems old and sick. Even if your parents have generally been open to living and working with others from different backgrounds, age may begin to affect their tolerance; many develop a strong preference for familiar people and surroundings, regardless of the opportunities or benefits this insular attitude may cost them.

Again, try to encourage your parents to be more open minded. But don't push too hard. If your parents feel they have no choice in the matter, or if you drive them into a stubborn and inflexible position, you run the risk of making them angry and depressed — or worse — compromising their self-esteem. This can be dangerous, for when people lose their feelings of self-worth, there isn't much left to live for.

Despite the imperfections in government services, however, you should explore what's available. It is important for your parent to apply for Medicaid, even if you think he or she is not eligible. Look for medical care, psychological and social support, transportation, housing, food, in-home nursing care and other programs. Expect to spend quite a bit of time just searching for the help your parents may need. The process of finding appropriate agencies, applying, qualifying and actually obtaining services for the first time can take six months to a year. Meanwhile, don't sit idle and wait. It's far better for the family to begin helping parents as needed. Then, over a period of time you can let government social service agencies supplement or replace the family's help.

Usually, the smartest course is to consider government agencies as just one component in the social, economic and medical support network you put together for your aging parents. Very few families find government agencies to be a complete source for their parents' daily living requirements.

Can Private Agencies Fill the Gaps?

Many adult children hope to help their aging parents by arranging for private services and support. Unfortunately, the availability of private agencies providing medical care, psychological and social support, transportation, housing, meals, or scheduled nursing care is fairly spotty. Most urban areas offer many of these specialized services for aging adults. But if you live in a small town, you're likely to find far fewer choices.

Private Services

However, the *range* of home-based services that can help your parents maintain an independent lifestyle is very broad.

Visiting Nurses or Home Health Nurses are usually registered or licensed vocational nurses who are specially trained to work in conjunction with a doctor's orders or prescriptions. They can visit regularly during recuperation after illness, accident, or discharge from a hospital, or can come to the home less frequently, but for a longer period of time to aid a person chronically ill. They monitor vital signs, give medication or injections, administer intravenous fluids, provide nutrition, change dressings, note any changes in physical or mental status and stay in communication with the doctor regarding treatment progress and plans. If the patient is terminally ill, a nurse can often provide hospice care in the home.

Social Workers visit primarily to perform physical and mental status examinations, and to evaluate living quarters with an eye for equipment and services an elderly person might require. They are trained to determine the help a person needs with basic daily activities, such as bathing, eating and getting around, and to arrange for access to appropriate services.

Physical Therapists follow a treatment plan established by a physician to maintain or improve a patient's physical capabilities. They teach the patient and family caregivers special exercise programs and how to handle any expected discomfort. They also monitor progress toward treatment goals, and report to the supervising physician.

Occupational Therapists assist disabled patients in acquiring or reacquiring daily living skills, and adapting to their disabilities. They evaluate the home for physical problems it may pose — such as difficulty opening the refrigerator, operating the stove, or climbing the stairs — and recommend adaptive devices to help your parent cope.

Respiratory Therapists treat breathing disorders according to the directions of a supervising physician, and help rehabilitate your parents after surgery.

Speech Therapists can work with the elderly at home to treat disorders affecting verbal communication, especially after a stroke.

Home Health Aides, Homemakers, or Attendants provide assistance with personal care, including grocery shopping, cooking and feeding, changing clothing and bed linens, laundry, bathing and other aspects of personal care. They can also provide light nursing care under supervision of a nurse or doctor.

Although each of these services may add to the cost of maintaining your parents in their own home, the arithmetic can still make sense when you include all the practical and intangible benefits of having your parents live independently. For everyone in the family, the moment when parents give up their independent lifestyle can mark the beginning of a long period of caregiving and worry. Moving your parents out of the familiar surroundings of their home can bring on physical and mental problems more rapidly. They may become depressed, allow themselves to become overly dependent, or shift to a lifestyle that makes heavy demands on everyone else in the family. In almost every case, parents who can maintain independent lifestyles live better, and also make life better for everyone else in the family.

Private Facilities

If your parents cannot continue to live entirely on their own, they can consider some form of semi-independent housing. These range from senior apartments to retirement hotels, board-and-care facilities, and various forms of shared or sheltered housing.

The private agencies which provide these services and support these facilities, like their counterpart government agencies, can be heavily squeezed by rising costs, a shortage of qualified nurses, aides and assistants, and countless problems of caring for ill, weak and deteriorating patients. Furthermore, many private agencies operate in older, over-crowded facilities.

Even so, there are probably several private agencies near you or your parents worth a close look. Don't rule out private services and residence programs, provided the family has the necessary financial resources or insurance to pay. However, don't fall into the trap of viewing private agencies as the perfect way to care for your aging parents. At best, they represent only one set of options that may — or may not — be suitable during a particular period of time.

Can Case Managers Stand In?

In some families, none of the adult children is in a good position to care for aging parents personally. By some estimates, as many as one third of adult children help care for parents who live hundreds or thousands of miles away. Most of these children have no choice, because they are established in distant cities with families of their own.

Some adult daughters and sons report they regularly travel 400, 600, even 1,000 miles several times a month to spend a day at a time chauffeuring their parents to doctors, shopping and other activities. Many more admit they tried this for a while, but had to give it up because of the costs and the strains on their own families and careers. Adult children can be very devoted and self-sacrificing in trying to keep up this long-distance commuting, but virtually all of them run out of steam eventually.

Distance isn't the only obstacle. Many others, even those who live within a few miles of their parents, simply don't have the time, temperament, or freedom to visit and care for them regularly. Too many other factors — demanding careers, busy families, a child's illness — can get in the way of personally giving your parents adequate care.

A practical alternative is to hire a professional case manager. Case managers often have backgrounds in nursing, social work, or other health professions. Working in the community where your parents live, a case manager essentially takes on the role of your "brother" or "sister" and does the things you'd do for your parents.

For a fee, the case manager assesses your aging parents and takes steps to set up resources and services to aid them. The case manager may help them locate a suitable place to live, furnish it and fit it with any necessary adaptive devices. He or she may help your parents shop for food, visit doctors, manage income, pay bills and establish a settled life. A good case manager can also find the right public agencies, private services, aides and others to help your parents clean house, prepare meals, maintain the home and care for personal needs, as required. Case managers can stay involved for years at a time. They will regularly visit your parents at home, in the hospital, or at a nursing home, verifying they are well cared for and socializing with them.

Good case managers tend to be warm, caring people. But they must also be professional and competent. Obviously, the case manager should be based near your parents, and should have a solid working knowledge of the social service agencies, medical facilities and other resources in the local area. You can find case managers through nursing homes, hospitals, physicians, or senior services agencies in your parents' community. A few advertise in the yellow pages or in newspapers and on radio. Word-of-mouth is the best reference. Ask friends and acquaintances about case managers they may know personally or may have heard about.

Be very careful in finally selecting a private case manager. This profession is largely unlicensed, unregulated, unrated and uncertified by professional, state, or federal authorities. Anyone can represent him- or herself as a case manager, and you will find little objective information on which to prove or disprove the claim. Check references and reputations, of course, but carefully consider and compare several case managers' skills, knowledge and personal style before you trust one with your parents' continued well-being. Afterwards, keep evaluating the quality of service the case manager provides.

Can You Help Your Parents?

So far, we've discussed several sources of assistance and support for your aging parents, but none of them replaces you and your brothers and sisters. Even if every public and private social service agency were fully funded and fully staffed, your parents would still do better to rely on you. There are too many health and safety concerns and other problems your parents won't overcome unless you're there to help. Regardless of what you believe, the adult children of aging parents cannot escape final responsibility. No matter how many available options you include in the total portfolio of help for your parents, ultimately you cannot pass the buck.

Here's something learned from personal experience, and confirmed by conversations with hundreds of other families: Caring for your aging parents is very much like caring for your children who become sick, injured, or otherwise needy. You don't like the situation. You may also regularly suffer conflict within yourself about your responsibilities as a caregiver. You wish it weren't necessary to give so much time and attention. You regret that it costs so much. You may feel anger, resentment, or even hatred toward the person you're safeguarding and supporting. But when all is said and done, you do as much as you possibly can.

The main difference when you're parenting your aging parents is that your parents are not children, so you must allow them considerably more independence and self-determination. There's usually more emotional baggage in the caregiving relationship, too, because you and your parents have had many years to build up strong feelings. The reversal of roles — from child to "parent" and parent to "child" — are very demanding experiences.

Though this responsibility may feel like a straightjacket today, it will lead to much better feelings in the long run. Your acceptance of responsibility will help your aging loved ones maintain a much better quality of life, even if you can't provide for all their needs single-handedly.

Self Torture

For most of the families interviewed, the worst part of taking primary responsibility for aging parents is not the day-to-day work. It's their own guilt and conflict over feeling anything less than a whole-hearted desire to help their parents. Unfortunately, very few people faced with heavy obligations realize how natural it is to want to run away and be free from the responsibility.

Of course, no amount of family stories or personal sagas will stop you from torturing yourself if you really must. But it is perfectly natural for even the best, most devoted adult children sometimes to wish their parents weren't so needy, weren't so demanding, weren't so much a part of their lives. In fact, the nicest, most civilized adult children in the world can wish their aged, suffering parents were dead.

But remember this: No lightning strikes when you have these thoughts and feelings. They're normal. Nothing bad or dangerous is caused by such sentiments. For most of us, these feelings are a part of the total experience of parenting our aged parents. It's wrong to punish yourself for having them, just as it's wrong to try avoiding them. The best course is to let the feelings come and wash over you. You're not going to act on them, and it's self-defeating to use them as an excuse to torture yourself emotionally.

Self Preservation

Many adult children neglect their own health and well-being while doing everything they can for their parents. Don't fall into this trap! While you're taking care of your parents, take good care of your own mental and physical health.

The best way to make sure you can help your parents over the long haul is to keep yourself mentally, physically and emotionally fit, and to continue your other relationships. Be careful to maintain your own life: home, family, work, school, friends and all the rest. Retain your healthy eating habits. Get ready for rapid-fire sequences of intense emotions, including helplessness, fear, anger, guilt and resentment. Regularly share your feelings — both good and bad — with others you love and trust. Talking about your feelings might not alleviate them entirely, but it will help prevent pent-up emotions from erupting into a new set of emotional or physical problems.

All too often adult children devote themselves to their parents and neglect all else. Frequently, this contributes more to weakening the caregiver than to sustaining the ones who need help.

Despite the relentless nature of your responsibilities toward your parents, make sure to leave yourself a reasonable amount of free time. Doing all you can to help your parents should not require super-human efforts or digging yourself an early grave. You can't nurture others all the time. It's healthy to get away from all your chores and burdens regularly for a day, a weekend, or longer. These respites will save your sanity, and they'll help you maintain a higher energy level so you can care for your parents longer and better.

Regardless of how much more you wish you could do, understand that whatever you accomplish for your parents is beneficial. No matter what anyone says (including your own inner voice), you're not required to solve all their problems. No one can give your parents a perfect life.

So do yourself a favor: Take satisfaction from the good you are able to do. Preserve yourself for the future by congratulating yourself on what you were able to accomplish today.

The Overbearing Child

Although there are good reasons for helping your parents, there's real danger in becoming too pushy. Just as it's bad policy to force others into helping, it's also unwise to force anyone into *receiving* help.

Look at it from your parents' point of view: How would you feel if a person came into your home and started changing things — especially when that person is your own child, now fully grown and apparently insensitive to what you want!

Just as you resented interference when you were young, your aging parents may resent your assumption of authority now. They may feel they can manage fairly well without your help, particularly if your intentions differ from theirs. Your overly intrusive attention may actually reduce their level of comfort and personal satisfaction.

In the Johnson family, for example, 83-year-old Rita merely needed an occasional ride to a doctor's appointment. But her son, Dan, and his wife, Sandra, spent several months trying to select her doctors, set up her appointments and personally administer her prescribed medicines. While sincerely trying to help, Dan and Sandra made doctors appointments at times that conflicted with Rita's previous arrangements with friends. Dan was bustling into his mother's life without noticing the havoc and distress he and his wife were creating. Rita tried to endure, but after several months she put her foot down. It took quite a family squabble for Rita to make clear to Dan and Sandra she wanted only a ride, not a pair of full-time nursemaids. There were some bad feelings on

both sides, and afterwards Rita felt drained and dissatisfied. It took more than a year before the family managed
to overcome the strain and hard feelings.

Managing a slow, steady and gentle transition toward
parental dependence on family assistance will go a long
way toward minimizing your parents' emotional adjustment to growing old and infirm. As in most families, you
will do your parents the most good if you tactfully offer
your help, but don't actually do anything for them until
they signal their willingness to let you.

Naturally, when parents are incapacitated, suddenly
struck with illness or injury, or otherwise suffering some
acute distress, you shouldn't worry about being too pushy.
When there are no other options, loving children may
"force" some assistance on their parents. In such
circumstances, your parents will almost always grateful-
ly accept the offer.

Even as your parents become more dependent,
remember they remain adults with legal and family
rights you must continue to honor. Work *with them* whenever possible to help them accomplish what they want. If
and when they begin to lose their faculties, you can
consider taking over and doing what you think is the best
for them. However, let events drive you to this position;
be careful not to rush there at the first opportunity.

When To Take Responsibility

When you face the responsibility of parenting your
children, you know exactly when to begin. There's a period
of pregnancy — or if you're adopting a child a period of
application, evaluation and waiting — followed by a
delivery. Suddenly, you have a child, and you're the
parent.

But when you're parenting your aging parents, the time to begin exercising your responsibilities is rarely so readily apparent. Occasionally a major illness, accident, or other crisis will signal the time for someone to help out. Much more often, your parents follow a slow, steady decline and gradually lose some of their self-sufficiency.

In some families, children are reluctant to face up to the problems of their aging parents. They may be afraid that once they begin to help out, there may be no end to their responsibility. They may also fear any weakness in Mom or Dad is a sign of impending death. But when adult children do start helping their parents, they usually find these fears were groundless. Most times, parents continue live quite well and happily for many, many years after they first need help. Family assistance directly improves their quality of life, takes some burdens from their shoulders, and shields them from stress that might otherwise accelerate their decline.

Symptoms of Decline

As they tire more easily and lose some of their mobility, your parents may begin to stay home more, forego their previous pleasures and lower their standards as they lose the ability to maintain a healthy, safe, satisfactory lifestyle. As their eyesight dims, their home may grow unsightly, dirty or dingy, and they may no longer be able to drive safely, particularly at night or in bad weather. (People over 65 have the worst injury and death rates per mile driven. Even though the vast majority still feel competent to drive, physical and mental abilities needed for driving do tend to deteriorate with advancing age.) As their mental faculties deteriorate, your parents may forget members of the family, stop bathing regularly, fail to prepare meals, and ignore broken or worn out appliances.

As they weaken with age, your parents may show other signs that they have begun a slow, downward spiral. They may have a harder time keeping up with dental and doctor visits, with diet and exercise requirements, with shopping, family visits and vacations or other trips. Minor and long-familiar annoyances such as noisy neighbors or a balky TV may begin to trigger much more anger or irritation. Gout, diabetes, circulation problems and other chronic conditions may begin to severely limit their mobility and opportunities to enjoy walks, family picnics and other favorite activities. Dentures may no longer fit, but your parents may not go to the trouble of getting them adjusted, and may try to get by eating only soft foods or liquids for long periods of time.

Aside from chronic or catastrophic illness or injury, there are many subtle symptoms that may signal you to consider offering your aging parents more help. Mom and Dad may not show all of them at once. The symptoms may come and go irregularly, or may appear with greater or lesser severity than described. Still, any one of these could be a warning sign:

- Sudden or gradual changes in personality, such as irritability or rapid mood swings, excessive sentimentality, loosening of inhibitions, impaired judgment.
- Lack of interest concerning family, friends and matters that once seemed very important.
- Lack of desire to leave the house.
- Depression, deep sadness, frequent tears, paranoia or mental delusions.

- Disorientation or loss of contact with reality, mental fabrications or hallucinations, rambling or incoherent speech.
- Loss of memory. Confusion about everyday matters, such as household bills and the names of family members.
- Wandering without a sense of direction.
- Physical symptoms of anxiety, such as palpitations, sweating, a lump in the throat.
- Excessive laxity in maintaining their home.
- Unsafe driving, sometimes indicated by a series of minor traffic violations or accidents.
- Changes in eating habits; dramatic weight loss.
- Changes in personal care, or in bladder and bowel habits and control.

A Guideline

One way to spot the appropriate time to begin parenting your aging parents is this: *Offer specific help when it will lead directly to an improvement in your parents' lives.* For example, Dan and Sandra Johnson still offer to drive Rita, their mother, to doctor's appointments or take her shopping for clothes. But where she can get along almost as well without them, as with cooking, walking and paying bills, they have learned to leave her alone.

This guideline helps prevent you from doing too much or making your parents more dependent than necessary. Following it, you can leave them more or less independent. At a certain point, your parents' general decline may progress far enough that your help becomes essential. Without it, your parents may have trouble maintaining a healthy, safe and satisfactory lifestyle. This is the time to consider making a long-term personal commitment.

You're Asked To Take Responsibility

Occasionally, someone outside the family will ask you to take more responsibility for your aging parents. A doctor or visiting nurse may call you to point out a serious physical problem or medical condition your parents apparently can't handle on their own, but which they haven't mentioned to you. If your parents lose control of their finances, you may be contacted by a bank, a creditor, or the IRS. Although being jolted this way by a family outsider is never pleasant, it can happen any time.

In the Gladstone family, for instance, Betty was shocked to receive a phone call from her mother's dressmaker about a bill that hadn't been paid in over six months. Betty questioned her mother, and discovered Willa Gladstone was paying the utilities, rent and insurance like clockwork, but had stopped paying many other bills. She had enough income to pay them, but had inexplicably lost interest in many of her ordinary responsibilities. Instead, she stuffed her unwanted bills in an old sewing box and pretended they didn't exist.

Betty was scared to learn this about her mother, who had always been so orderly and responsible. She called a family conference, and with the help of Jack and Dotty, her brother and sister, got their mother to agree to let Betty help once a month with paying bills, writing checks and keeping financial records. Now when Betty visits her mother, she checks the house thoroughly for unpaid bills. She keeps a list of regular payments, and has advised people like the dressmaker to send her duplicates of her mother's bills.

Your Parents Ask for Help

In many families, aging parents will ask their children for help point blank. In others, however, the request will come more subtly, between the lines, and family members must pay close attention to recognize it.

In the Williams family, Addison — long retired from his work as a CPA — began subtly asking for help by questioning his wife, Mildred, and his adult children about the details of new tax laws. Because he had always known much more than they about the laws, the family alertly realized Addison might be having trouble coping in other areas as well. They were right. A medical check-up revealed large gaps in Addison's memory.

Now that they know about Addison's increasingly frequent memory lapses, Mildred and the others are able to make his situation less distressing. They'll frequently remind Addison of who and what they're talking about, repeating the names of people they're mentioning in place of "he" or "she," and using full descriptive phrases like "tomorrow night's ball game" rather than referring to "it." They also remind Addison of previous conversations, and have learned to treat his forgetfulness casually so he doesn't become alarmed and anxious.

Something similar could happen in your family. Most often, parents begin telling long, involved stories that let you know they are having daily difficulties they never had before. Your father may complain he can't keep up with his hobby or his investments any longer. Your mother may lament she can't stay on her feet long enough to do the weekly grocery shopping. Whether they tell you about their car needing repair at a shop several miles from home, ask your advice about a financial opportunity, or call you at midnight with a sudden medical problem, your parents are letting you know they feel some loss of independence. You must be alert to these signals and offer your help.

You Can't Stand the Way Things Are

Many aging parents are too proud, too stubborn, or too unaware of their own diminished capacities ever to ask their adult children for help, directly or indirectly. In these situations, circumstances may ask you to help much more eloquently than your parents can.

For example, Fred Hinckley, age 82, with legs weakened by a childhood bout with polio, lived with his wife in a house full of steps. Up through his seventies, he was able to negotiate the flights of stairs. But as he grew older, he lost much of the strength in his legs and became virtually housebound. A stairway elevator between the first and second floors of the house helped him get around inside his home. But the dozen or so steps from the front door down to the street became too much of an obstacle. For a while, he managed occasional outings, mostly when family members would actually carry him down to the street. But as time passed, the old man endured two years without once leaving the house, even to see a doctor or dentist.

Fred was never one to ask for help. He remained housebound without many complaints until his daughter Jan noticed him sadly gazing out the front window at people walking by. She talked with her mother, then decided to help her aging parents move to an elevator building with easier entry and exit.

Now Fred could easily go outside in his wheelchair, sit with acquaintances, visit family members and accompany his wife to the neighborhood stores. Nevertheless, there was never any discussion of the move or the improvements it had brought. Fred's only way of saying "thank you" was to raise no objections.

Whether the problem is chronic and getting worse, like Fred's, or appears very suddenly, learn to expect that your parents will grow more dependent on help from others. Don't be too surprised when you first begin to feel dissatisfied with your parents' present living arrangements. If your parents need help but don't ask for it, you may have to make some or all of the effort to improve the situation on your own initiative.

Prepare a Plan in Advance

Your parents may live for many more years before they actually need help maintaining their health, safety, financial security, or quality of life. Nevertheless, it's a good idea to begin preparing for that day right now.

A good first step is to talk with your parents about the possibilities that lie ahead. Don't think this will be easy. Aging and possible physical or mental debilitation are never pleasant subjects for parents or their adult children. It commonly requires several attempts to get past the denial and discomfort you and they may feel. However, it's imperative to discover what they think, feel and want while they are still lucid enough to know and to tell you. The process of trying to talk about these important matters also makes the problems somewhat easier to accept and resolve when they begin to appear.

Try to find out exactly what your parents would like you to do in the event they become unable to manage their own affairs — whether through hospitalization, accident, or sudden illness. You should discuss their preferences among important medical, social, domestic and financial options. Learn the names of the doctors and other professionals they rely on. If they don't have any, recommend or at least discuss some names.

Perhaps most important, openly acknowledge the possibility that someone eventually may have to help your parents maintain a good quality of life. Your parents probably will have as hard a time swallowing the idea of dependence as you do, so the sooner and more frankly you first bring it up, the easier it will be for them to digest when there's no alternative.

Many aging parents actively resist this kind of talk. So be patient, but persistent. Don't let these subjects become taboo. Keep bringing them up, if only quickly and in general terms. Eventually, your parents will acknowledge these concerns and give you some guidance on how to make choices should they lose control over their own lives.

Another useful course of action (that doesn't require any cooperation from your parents) is to think about what might happen when your parents become more dependent on you. What will it mean for your daily life? For theirs? How much responsibility will you be willing to accept? How much will they be willing to relinquish? What help will they need? What kinds? How much help will you be able to give? Where will they get the rest of the services and support they need? What will be their financial resources and obligations? What about yours?

You won't have all the answers right away. But every moment you spend considering these questions will help you prepare both psychologically and emotionally for the demands of parenting your aging parents.

As you and your parents become more comfortable with the idea that they will probably need some help in the future, you'll want to begin investigating.

Look at your aging parents' housing. Is it adaptable to physical disabilities, to mental deterioration or incapacity? Is it affordable, convenient and pleasant enough to satisfy your parents? Can you find them a better living arrangement, closer to shopping and transportation?

Identify "para-transit" services in the community. These are on-call, low-cost transportation services made available to seniors and handicapped in order to help keep them more independent.

Consider financial security. Do your parents have enough financial resources to support the lifestyle they want? What is their outlook for income and expenses? What options do they have to maintain or improve their financial situation without undue risk? If they are suddenly disabled or taken ill, what provisions have they made for someone to manage their affairs, pay their bills and oversee the quality of their lives and the disposition of their estates? You might want to begin drawing up any necessary documents [see Chapter 3 (Finances)] and have them signed so they're ready to go into effect without delay.

If you're lucky, you'll be able to complete a cohesive plan before your parents need a great deal of caregiving. You can make it highly detailed or simply a strategic overview, but cover at least the vital areas of concern for your aging parents: alternatives for maintaining their health, safety, financial security and living arrangements. Have some clear ideas of the options your parents and others in your family might regard as acceptable and unacceptable in each of these areas. Try to get some agreement to the plan from everyone in your family before your parents' situation becomes urgent and events begin to buffet your emotions. When you eventually begin helping your parents, you naturally won't have to follow the plan in every detail. But you'll greatly appreciate having a solid basis from which to work.

CHAPTER 2

HOUSING

To Stay or To Move?

As your parents continue to age, one fundamental part of their lifestyle that may have to change is where they live. For most parents in their later years, the family home becomes too large, too old and too expensive to maintain. When this happens, many parents — including those who so far haven't needed any help from their adult children — choose to sell. They move to a better climate, a smaller condo or apartment that's easier to maintain, a newer and more convenient neighborhood, or some combination.

In more troublesome situations, parents don't move out. Instead, they hang on and suffer. They begin losing their ability to climb stairs, walk or drive. They may have trouble managing long trips to and from their home, maintaining the home, or handling other ordinary acts of daily life. They may complain that their neighborhood is running down. Although they tell you about their problems, they won't agree to move away from them. Your parents may feel tied to the house by economics — prefer-

ring a low or paid-off mortgage to much higher rental or
mortgage payments for any new home. Or they may need
or want the security of familiar surroundings, no matter
how difficult it is to live there.

Yet life can be made relatively easy for parents with
physical or mental disabilities. All it takes is a home
designed to support and compensate for them. Your
parents can either upgrade their present home, or move
to an upgraded one.

Helping your parents move to a new home can be
arduous, emotionally demanding, expensive and time
consuming. The choice of where to live is never an easy
one, especially for aging parents. Parents who have lived
in one place for a long time can feel strong ties to their
present home or neighborhood. They can worry about any
consideration of a move, and find good reasons — beyond
plain stubbornness — to resist any notion of moving away.

Parents are usually not the only ones with emotional
ties to a well-established family home. The idea of parents
moving out can upset other family members as well. To
brothers and sisters with vivid memories of life there, the
move can signal "the end of an era." On an emotional level,
at least, many children and grandchildren will take the
move as a clear sign the family's mainstays are giving
way. Few people are happy to see or accept such dramatic
changes.

Your parents may resist a move for other reasons.
They may see it as an admission they are growing older
and weaker. They may not want to change their lifestyle
to fit this new reality. In a growing number of families,
parents are mentally impaired or confused just enough so
they can't readily evaluate or comprehend the need to
move. Parents may also resist a move because it marks
the first time they must ask their adult children for help.
This can damage their self-esteem, and the emotional

whirlwind created can further complicate the ordinary practical problems of moving any long-established household.

Most commonly, your parents will want help selecting a new place, making the financial arrangements and physically moving their household goods. In families where the parents don't ask, family members usually offer their help and wind up getting involved in the move some way or another.

Regardless of whether or not your parents resist the idea of moving, there are some important logistical problems to consider. Your parents may not be physically able to drive or otherwise look for a new home. If your parents are handicapped, ill, or otherwise incapacitated, they may have no way to move their possessions without considerable help and expense. What's more, the direct costs of moving are often only the start, with rent or mortgage payments on the new place taking a big bite out of their budget.

Moving may also entail some practical disappointments. For example, when Fred Hinckley and his wife moved to an elevator apartment, his adult children and their families had to give up access to his large house in a good location. Many family homes have special amenities that relatives greatly appreciate, such as a large backyard or a dining room that accommodates the whole family. Some homes are a family's best investment, and selling it for health reasons may lead to an untimely sale at too low a price.

Another source of emotional distress comes when aging parents who are moving out of the family home try to distribute or give away their family heirlooms, such as special china, silverware, and furniture, and their other possessions, such as power tools, excess clothing, trophies and other memorabilia. Such distributions make a great deal of practical sense, since the new home may have no space for the items, and parents planning to cut down on entertaining and other activities may have no use for them. However practical it may be, distributing personal and household treasures among loved ones contributes to an emotional climate of finality that can shake younger members of the family. No one should pretend these feelings do not exist.

Whether your parents are completely comfortable in their present home or looking to move next week, housing is a fundamental factor that contributes significantly to their quality of life. Where they live and how well it suits them should be one of the first things you consider in helping them remain as comfortable, happy and functional as possible. If they're safe and satisfied in their present home, that's fine, although you may want to plan for the future. If they're not, there are many alternatives to explore.

Criteria for Living Arrangements

Your parents can choose from a tremendous number of options in selecting where they will live. But making the best choice is rarely easy. They will have to evaluate the basic features of different homes, apartments and other living spaces, and consider many specific details. They may need your help in considering the most important factors like location, amenities, design, convenience, spaciousness and cost. Your parents may also want to weigh other important details: whether appliances are electric or gas, the amount and location of closet space, the new location's proximity to shopping and transportation, and so forth.

Another consideration in choosing where to move will often be the new neighbors. Certain communities or neighborhoods are geared to singles, others to families with young children, and still others to seniors. Retirement hotel residents are usually much more vigorous and capable than patients in nursing homes, but more dependent than residents in apartment or condo complexes. Your parents' ideas on who they want as neighbors can significantly influence their range of choices.

What's more, your parents are unique individuals with their own needs, preferences and idiosyncrasies. Chances are, their first choice in housing won't be the one you would pick to live in. If they're limited for any reason to less-than-perfect choices, there's no telling what problems or deficiencies they'll be most willing to tolerate.

In the Morgan family, Fern, one of the adult daughters with her own husband and family, recently moved her parents from the East Coast to the West Coast. The plan was to sell the family home and buy the parents a condo near Fern. But after listing everything her parents wanted, carefully investigating a dozen locations and finally identifying the best condo complex, Fern couldn't buy any of the units in time for Claude and Velma's arrival. In the last desperate days before they arrived, Fern found her parents an apartment in a complex advertised as "short term" corporate housing. She meant it to be only a stopgap place to stay. But once they moved in, Claude and Velma found scores of retired, older couples who had lived there steadily for more than a dozen years! They loved their new home. When they visited the condo complex Fern had selected, they hated it on sight. Fern accepted their decision easily, and felt grateful that by sheer luck she had found her parents a wonderful place to live. If she had bought them the condo she *thought* they would like, Fern realized, Claude and Velma would have been very unhappy living there.

Aside from personal preferences, there are five sets of specific, tangible factors you'll want to evaluate in helping your parents decide where they should live. These factors don't change much whether you're checking over the old family farm or glancing through a vacation apartment your parents may wish to occupy for a few weeks.

Physical safety

Is the home a safe place for your parents to live? Check for reasonable precautions and safety features to prevent or discourage fire, theft and other obvious dangers. For example, you wouldn't want to see your parents living at the bottom of a steep grade in a mobile home that is regularly rammed by eighteen-wheelers over the years. Neither would you want your parents living with broken glass outside their door, piles of newspapers next to an open flame cooktop, or windows and doors that can't be locked. Homes should be secure, with good outdoor and indoor lighting, smoke detectors throughout, and well maintained heating and hot water systems. If there is a second floor, you'll want a safe exit from there to the ground in case of a stairwell fire.

Location

Although few families have the money to live wherever they like, they should nevertheless look carefully at a home's surroundings and neighborhood. Think about the quality of life there. Consider, for example, crime and personal safety in the neighborhood. Some neighborhoods today are battlefields, while others are very safe. It's desirable to have shopping, medical and other basic services nearby, as well as public transportation, a library, movies or other entertainment, and a senior center, community center, church or other social gathering place.

Distance

Few adult children want to live right next door to their parents. But in helping your parents evaluate a home, you might want to factor in the time and trouble it takes to travel there and back. During a busy week, you might enjoy a pleasurable family outing to Grandma's, but not if it requires an hour-long ride through heavy traffic. Should you ever have to make frequent trips at odd hours to provide help, a long ride might become a source of irritation and resistance. More important: if Mom or Dad ever faces an emergency, your travel time could make a significant difference in the outcome, and in how you would feel afterwards about the help you were able to provide.

There are other important advantages to close proximity. When grandparents live in the neighborhood, they can more easily visit and babysit, and can receive young teenagers who ride their bikes over to visit. In almost every way, reducing the miles between you and your parents takes some of the time and trouble out of lending a helping hand.

Personal convenience

Inside their dwelling, you want to see enough room for your parents to move around freely, but not so much they feel dwarfed by the interior spaces or overwhelmed by the upkeep. You'll want your parents to have ample work space and room for the tools, materials and pastimes they enjoy, whether they love to cook, collect stamps, or build furniture. Many aging parents cannot conveniently climb stairs, and will have to live on one floor at ground level or in an elevator building. You should also consider practical matters, such as proximity to parking for carrying groceries and other frequent burdens, and the location of the washer and dryer. Must they go outdoors to do their laundry? How far? How safe is the location? How will they carry their laundry to and from the machines?

If your parents have handicaps, see if you can make changes to prevent their home from becoming a straight-jacket. For example, people confined to a wheelchair need lower counter-tops and appliances, ramps and wide doorways. They may need handgrips in bathrooms, and perhaps a bath lift to help them bathe or shower. Those with poor eyesight may need bright lights and color coding throughout their house or apartment. People suffering from Alzheimer's Disease often benefit from large clocks and calendars, labeled doors and drawers, and double-cylinder locks on exit doors to help prevent wandering. A recent report from the Commonwealth Fund's Commission on Elderly People Living Alone showed some 5.5 million elderly Americans, including about 1.6 million with severe disabilities or impairments, living comfortably at home using adaptive devices like these to compensate for their handicaps.

Buy versus Rent

Financial considerations can make your parents much more interested in either buying or renting their next home. The advantages of buying include: price appreciation, tax advantages, freedom to renovate and remodel, and relatively fixed housing costs. But your parents may prefer the advantages of renting: relative freedom from maintenance and other responsibilities, flexibility to move again and no large investment.

In some families, parents feel a strong preference for one alternative despite strong financial pressures to do the opposite. If your parents decide to explore only one alternative, they automatically limit their range of housing choices. Claude and Velma Morgan's daughter, Fern, didn't look at some of the most desirable rental complexes occupied mainly by seniors, because her parents had wanted to buy. Similarly, had she known they would ultimately be happy renting, she wouldn't have wasted her few spare hours looking for a home they could purchase.

Probably the best approach to helping your parents consider a move is to encourage them to proceed — but cautiously. Your parents should talk to a few people living in a particular complex or neighborhood before deciding to move in. The family should evaluate each option carefully before making any decisions. Aging parents often need time to experience their new home before they know how well it suits them. They should also bear in mind that their physical needs and limitations may change. Although they may have few options, encourage your parents not to buy a home until they feel sure of how and where they want to live. Should they rent, encourage them to keep their legal and financial commitments relatively short-term.

Your Parents Can Live Where They Are

Unless your parents moved in with you years ago, they probably have a place of their own. Only about five percent of people over age 65 live with their families, and only another five percent live in nursing homes. The remainder live with their spouse, alone, or in specialized housing for seniors, like board-and-care or retirement hotels. Your parents are likely to stay put, too, unless there's a sudden and compelling reason to move. Only about one percent of those over age 60 move their place of residence in a given year. Even when they move, most aging Americans continue to live independently or semi-dependently. So when evaluating where your parents should live, the obvious place to start is where they are now.

Although the family home was probably a great place at one time, over the years it can become less desirable. The neighborhood today may be entirely changed from when your parents first moved in. If the neighborhood has stayed the same, your parents may have changed. They may want different kinds of neighbors or amenities. If they live in the city, they may no longer want to take a subway to the supermarket. Older parents dwelling in the country may not want to keep stoking the wood-burning stove. Stairways are often a compelling reason to move — fatigue, injury or illness make stairs much less acceptable than before.

Joanne and Carl Thompson had lived in their large home for over thirty years. During the last few years, their neighborhood had begun to grow seedy, and all their friends and family had moved ten miles or more to suburban areas. Gilbert and Alisha, their adult children, had steadily urged their parents to move somewhere closer so they could live an easier life and see the grandchildren more. But Joanne and Carl were stubborn — and somewhat afraid of a change. Eventually, though, Joanne suffered a stroke and could no longer manage the stairs to the second-floor bedroom. Carl had been holding out against a move, though keeping the big house warm in the winter cost more than he wanted. But after Joanne's stroke, he quickly gave in and the pair moved to a comfortable condominium just five minutes from their adult children. Within three months, they were completely happy in their new home and openly regretted not moving earlier.

Home Improvements

Even if your parents are suffering in their present home, they need not move right away. Many parents who once had trouble living comfortably in their present home find they can stay for many more years after their adult children help them remedy major deficiencies or arrange for key supplementary services. A few simple, small changes will often let your parents live comfortably without moving.

One important improvement can be arranging for the use of "para-transit" services in the community. These are on-call, low-cost transportation services for senior citizens (and for handicapped — many are equipped with wheelchair lifts). Your parents can call and arrange for a ride to shopping, medical appointments and other commitments with friends and family any time during business hours, and sometimes during extended hours. They can remain relatively independent without the risk of climbing behind the wheel of a car and without the nuisance or embarrassment of relying on someone in the family to act as chauffeur.

Parents with hearing problems can benefit from door-bells, smoke alarms and alarm clocks that use lights to supplement sound. You can add an amplifier to their telephone, and install a telecommunication device that substitutes printed words for voice conversations. Many television shows are broadcast with "closed captions" that appear on the screen if your parents hook their TV to a special decoding device.

If your parents have vision deficiencies, they can install brighter lights, a large-screen TV (with the added convenience of remote control), large-dial clocks, and reflective tape or other warnings for stairwells and low doorways. They can also strategically place ticking clocks or other noise makers to serve as location markers and guideposts.

If they have mobility problems, you can install strong handgrips at important points throughout their home. You can also get them to use a walker, cane, or wheelchair. When one or both parents use a wheelchair, make sure anywhere they stay has street access and relatively wide doorways, particularly into a bathroom. If necessary, you can remodel their kitchen and bathroom to provide easier access, lower sinks and other improvements. One good idea when your parents are handicapped or partially immobilized is to remove all the throw rugs and other obstacles to easy movement. It's free, and it works! A good way to test for less obvious obstacles is to explore your parents' home with your eyes closed, or to roll around in Mom's or Dad's wheelchair. Try to get to the bathroom, the kitchen, the front door, and so forth. Your new perspective may help you notice problems that surprise you.

If parents lose lifting power in their legs, you can easily install compensating devices, such as chair lifts and stairway elevators. Most medical supply stores sell inexpensive handrails you can easily attach to fit around any toilet. A special seat can raise any toilet six, eight, or ten inches to accommodate handicapped parents. For bathing or showering, a pivoting "bath lift" can support your parent in a stall shower or ride him or her smoothly up and down into a bath tub. The device installs easily and uses water pressure from the tap for lifting and lowering, so there's no risk of electric shock. They can also benefit from handgrips and an inexpensive shower seat. Another nice convenience is a hand-held showerhead, which installs easily in any tub or shower.

It's a good idea for your parents to put telephone jacks in every room of their home, so they won't have to walk far, or rush to answer. Extra phones are relatively inexpensive, as is extra baseboard wiring to reach all the rooms. If wiring is impractical, a cordless telephone can work almost anywhere.

One potentially life-saving convenience is "speed dialing" — a way to make a telephone call by pushing only one or two buttons on the telephone. This service is available from local telephone companies for a monthly charge. You can also buy a telephone with an automatic dialer. Help your parents program important telephone numbers, such as their doctor, police and fire departments, a dentist and taxi service. Add your own telephone number, as well as the apartment manager or a responsible neighbor, and friends or family your parents call frequently. Your parents may want a telephone with extra large pushbuttons for easier dialing. Also, post a list of important names and telephone numbers close to the phone, where ambulance attendants called to help your parents in an emergency can pick it up and use it. Some communities have formal "Medic Alert" programs, but you can provide much the same security with a list itemizing all your parents' medications that you post prominently in their home.

You can also install a Personal Emergency Response System, or pager. With it, your parents can easily summon police, fire, or emergency medical assistance from anywhere in or around their home. These systems generally have callstations installed throughout the dwelling. Your parents can activate one with the touch of a button. They can also trigger a call for help with a pocket-size remote control they can carry. In lieu of installing an emergency response system, you can see that your parents place a telephone on a low chair or table, close enough to the floor for them to crawl over and use if they fall for any reason and can't get up.

Visit a medical equipment showroom or browse through a catalog to see the variety of ingenious devices you can use to improve your aging parents' day-to-day living. For most families, helping parents meet the requirements of living independently for as long as possible costs much less and provides better quality of life than confining them to an institution.

Hiring Help

Another approach to make your parents' present home more livable is to hire someone to help them with daily chores and responsibilities, and to be a companion. This can be a full-time job, of course. Yet someone who works just two or three hours a day, two or three days a week can produce an important difference in your parents' lifestyle. If you try this approach, investigate carefully. Make sure of the hours this person will be available, and whether they are making a long-term or short-term commitment. If you're working with an employment agency, find out whether it is bonded and insured.

You can also consider setting up regular visits by a qualified home health aide or by other health professionals. These visits are usually easy to arrange through community agencies, and go a long way toward increasing your parents' safety and quality of life in their present home. You can line up any combination of community-based nutrition services, volunteer "friendly visitors," home-delivered meals, telephone reassurance services, and membership in a nearby senior center where your parents can meet others and pursue interesting activities.

The net result can be considerable improvement in the "livability" of your parents' present home.

Begin looking for helpful resources by contacting the Commission on Aging or another umbrella organization in your area. Look in the telephone book under "Aging" or "Senior Services." (To get you started, there's a Resource Guide in the back of this book which includes national and state agencies and organizations concerned with aging. You can obtain an updated list directly from the publishers by sending a stamped, self addressed envelope.) These resources can help you find a broad range of assistance in your community, including:

Home health services from visiting nurses, home health aides, physical therapists, speech therapists, occupational therapists, or social workers and "respite" caregivers who temporarily assume your caregiving responsibilities;

Homemaker services from day or live-in companions, visiting homemakers, home-delivered meal programs, or chore services;

Life enhancement services from transit and para-transit organizations, senior adult day centers, social clubs, volunteer programs, hobby and special interest groups, or "reassurance" visiting or telephone calling groups;

Home medical equipment and supplies from durable medical equipment dealers who offer oxygen equipment, ventilators, beds and wheelchairs, lifts, incontinence supplies and much more.

Also, look for religious and community organizations that may provide services of benefit to your parents. In many neighborhoods, much of the social service burden is borne by churches, synagogues and other community organizations rather than by specialized government agencies. These programs can be easier to access, as well as warmer and more supportive than bureaucratic environments. In addition, local clergy can often provide a great deal of emotional support, practical advice and contact information when your parents need help.

Once you make a good set of arrangements, don't ignore the need for "back up." For example, when Gilbert and Alisha Thompson hire a person to help care for their aging parents, Carl and Joanne, they always determine how easily they can get replacement help if the aide calls in sick or is otherwise unavailable for a day or a week. If the hired person takes a leave of absence or quits entirely, the Thompson family has a serious problem, so they maintain a contingency plan. Some adult children prefer to set up several arrangements, such as hiring two part-time workers instead of one, or arranging for several different types of visitors on different schedules. This can ease the problems of getting someone on short notice to help your parents at a particular time and date.

You may also wish to find out if your parents' government or private insurance will pay some or all of the cost of outside services and hired help. In most cases, insurance covers only direct medical expenses, such as health aids, adaptive devices and treatments prescribed by a doctor.

Despite everything you do, however, some homes become unsuitable. If this happens to your parents, here are some alternative living options:

Your Parents Can Live With You

If your parents can no longer live in their present home, or become incapable of living independently, or if one parent dies and the other cannot live alone, one alternative usually is to move in with you or another family member. This can save money, and simplify problems of care-giving and health maintenance.

You may want to choose this course if you have a large home where your parents can live without crowding your own family, or if family finances are too tight to pay for all the service and support they would need to live alone. In a growing number of families, pooling aging parents' and adult children's money is a good way to get a better and more spacious home than either household could afford separately.

In the Williams family, for example, Mildred and Addison's increasing forgetfulness made their adult daughter Greta and her husband, Bill Ford, worry about the older couple's safety. When Bill and Greta began looking for a larger house for themselves, they persuaded Mildred and Addison to move in with them. With the extra money Mildred and Addison contributed to the household budget, the extended family bought a large, old farmhouse. It had a delightful, separate "apartment" where Mildred and Addison could maintain their privacy. Yet they were part of the household, so Bill and Greta could help them maintain a good quality of life without too much extra effort.

Studies and personal recollections show many aging grandparents greatly enjoy the opportunity to live with babies and young children. More than living nearby, living in the same household welds the family even closer together. Both the oldest and youngest family members can get needed stimulation from the arrangement. For the adult children in the "sandwich generation," having Mom or Dad around to help with the children — provided they're able — can also bring some welcome relief from daily pressures and responsibilities.

When Parents Move In

Many families, however, still consider parents moving in with adult children as the option of last resort. There are several significant problems that can come up when parents move in.

First, strong family feelings usually begin to come out in rather loud tones. Parents and adult children who live together seem to fight regularly over everything from politics and money to eating habits and housekeeping concerns. Most families have profound generational differences concerning everything from division of labor to value systems and who gets the comfortable chair.

Grandchildren can be another point of contention. Grandparents often feel they have a constitutional right to overrule their adult children on child-rearing matters — or at least to ignore whatever rules the grandchildren are expected to follow. Most times, this results in relatively benign transgressions: too much candy, too many toys, and so forth. Yet with everyone living under the same roof, sparks can fly for little reason, particularly when grandchildren are disciplined — or when they're not.

Your parents' own emotional turmoil can also lead to problems. They may go through periods of feeling dependent and more helpless than ever. They may resent everything that reminds them of their weakened condition. When they move in with their adult children, parents are putting a burr under their own saddles. Everything about the home, the meals, the daily schedule, the sleeping arrangements, the financial situation and all the rest is likely to irritate them at one time or another. Many aging parents and their adult children have developed warm and loving relationships while living together, yet many others have suffered emotional trauma and distress trying to live as an ideal extended family.

Most thirty to sixty year olds find that bringing their parents home to live can be demanding and disruptive. Even when problems don't actually materialize, there may be a strain as household members try hard to get along. Whether parents are rapidly deteriorating or just in danger of future problems, adult children may feel reluctant to go on vacation or business trips, or simply enjoy a night out by themselves. Even the most loving and devoted adult children may find that caring for their parents at home can create problems of privacy and unwanted interference in the most intimate matters.

For example, Connie Abboud urgently wanted Carol and Edward, her aging mother and father, to move in with her and her husband, Vasile, and their three children. Connie and Vasile's house had an extra bedroom and bathroom that would give Carol and Edward a fair amount of privacy. After much discussion, they finally moved in. At first, the arrangement worked well because Connie was easily able to care for her father's chronic diabetes and her mother's poor blood circulation.

But after a year of having her parents in her home, Connie began to develop a strong resentment for the way her father treated her mother. Edward and his son-in-law Vasile argued regularly over household finances, and Carol began meddling in her daughter's relationship with Vasile and the children. Connie remembered her parents as pillars of maturity and strength. She was shocked they could be so petty and childish. Rather than ignore her own emotional needs and resign herself to the role of everyone's mother, Connie decided Carol and Edward had to find their own place. During a family discussion, Carol and Edward made clear they also wanted to move. A month or two later, they found an apartment only a few blocks away. Almost immediately, the family relationships returned to normal, and they still have the pleasure of spending time and helping each other whenever they wish.

If you're uncomfortable with harsh feelings toward your parents, you have plenty of company. Many adult children feel they must actually enjoy the process of caring for their parents. They don't like to admit living with their parents is a strain and a pain — even when it is. Many more adult children feel a strong conflict: They'd like to keep their parents out, but they feel there's no other adequate choice, so they invite their parents to move in — and grow to resent it.

Don't bother working toward sainthood; few attain it. Conflict and mixed emotions are normal, particularly when you're parenting your aging parents. You can't get rid of these feelings completely. Instead, you must honestly explore them. That's the only way to become comfortable with them. Consider whether you really want them to move in. Try to anticipate both the good and bad aspects of having your parents live with you, and don't presume what feels right for you is right for everyone. Be careful not to expect too much from this living arrangement unless everyone involved honestly expresses enthusiasm for it.

Keeping Peace in the Household

If the family decides your parents can and should live with you, here are some ideas that can help you reduce the stress and improve relationships:

Establish and maintain a household routine for basic chores and responsibilities. Include everything from preparing meals and cleaning up to doing laundry, shopping for food, and all the rest. Because you're likely to feel a lot of pressure after your parents move in, allow for plenty of rest periods and "quiet times." This gives every-one in the household a chance to cool down and relax.

Make sure everyone has suitable living quarters and at least a measure of privacy when needed. If your parents move in with you, your own children may have to "double up" to make more room. This can create its own special pressures — but advantages, too. Many children who room together develop especially close relationships. The younger one matures a little faster; the older one feels a little more responsible.

But any time people are crowded together with little or no privacy, there's plenty of potential for high emotion. If your house doesn't have enough room for privacy, try to create or improve an outdoor sitting area. Make some provision so everyone in the household can find a place to be alone once in a while — even if the best you can manage is sending your parents "out" with other relatives or friends one evening a month.

Clearly establish who is the head of the household, and agree on each person's responsibilities. Even Grandma and Grandpa can have chores to do and limits on their freedom and authority. Two "Dads" or two "Moms" living in one house can easily make the sparks fly. You'll have a much better time together once you work out these power relationships. Start *before* your parents move in. Keep working toward improvements until the situation is satis-factory. If you ignore these issues, expect some serious head-butting as long-established habits and preferences come into conflict.

Make an effort to keep your parents' presence from disrupting other relationships within the household. For example, don't let Grandma prevent Mom from scolding the grandchildren for dumping chocolate pudding on the rug or getting poor grades in school. Don't let Grandpa tell Dad about all the mistakes he's making in bringing up his children or handling his business affairs. People in the "sandwich generation" may have a lot of trouble with the myriad of conflicting pressures and responsibilities concerning their parents and their children.

Maintain your own identity as a family. Plan special times for you and your own children. Grandparents need not be included in everything you do. The time away from your aging parents will not only give you a breather from responsibilities, but will help everyone feel better when you rejoin them later.

Encourage your parents to maintain their own life-style and to exercise a reasonable amount of independence. Let your parents bring as much furniture, clothing and other objects into your home as seems practical. Encourage them to prepare some of their own meals, entertain their own friends and make their own transportation plans using outside services, friends, or other relatives. If they have their own sitting area, for example, your parents can much more easily establish their own schedules for TV, visitors and other daily activities. Everyone in a household benefits when parents live more as "boarders" than "dependents." But let the situation develop at its own pace. If you put pressure on your parents to be too independent, or if you restrict them needlessly, you may ultimately do more harm than good.

Obtain whatever special equipment your parents need to make living in your home more comfortable. Many of the same items you could install in their own home will also be appropriate when they live with you. [See "Home Improvements" earlier in this Chapter.] If you think a special device will help, get one as soon as possible. If it doesn't work, you can always sell it and try a different approach. If you're uncertain, you can usually rent such equipment for a period and check its usefulness in daily service. In some cases, your parents' government or private insurance may pay some or all of the bill for this kind of "medical equipment," particularly with proper prescriptions from a physician.

Make sure everyone treats your parents pleasantly, and with respect. Even within the family, "thank you" and "please" are words for everyone to use as often as possible. Make a strong effort to show your parents how much you care about them. If you treat them like a burden, they'll almost certainly feel unhappy about living with you. Despite any medical or emotional problems your parents may face, don't let the household mood stay morbid, resentful, or angry. There are always family events and activities to enjoy and celebrate. Try hard to make the time your parents spend with you happy and warm.

Carefully monitor your parents' health, and seek medical or other help before a small problem becomes a big emergency. Although your parents may seem fairly strong and healthy, their age puts them at risk for sudden decline. If a child lingers with a cold, there may be no real cause for alarm. But if your aging parent does, it may warrant a visit to a doctor. Get to know your parents' doctor, dentist and other medical professionals. Keep in touch with them so you're ready to discuss potentially significant changes in Mom or Dad as soon as they occur.

Encourage everyone in the family to talk about the live-in arrangement before it begins and as it develops. Hidden feelings, fears and uncertainties fester and grow into unreasonable problems and expectations. It's simpler and better to openly discuss your parents' requirements, their physical and emotional conditions, and the household disruption they may cause. However, don't dwell on problems. Mix discussions of problems with talk of pleasures, and with other household conversation.

Allow for a long period of adjustment. Young children may adapt to the new living arrangement much quicker than others, and your parents may be the last to accept the new household arrangement. Expect many emotional flare-ups and conflicts after your parents first move in. These are normal. As long as everyone in the family tries hard to remain tolerant and loving, and as long as progress continues toward household peace, you can feel confident the living arrangement is probably working. If your family doesn't face problems, someone is probably hiding something.

Your Parents Can Live Semi-Independently

In many families, it's simply unworkable for parents to move in with an adult child. The problems may stem from money pressures, a shortage of living space, too many demands by the adult child's career or family, personality conflicts, or another solid cause. There's no stigma in deciding your parents can't live with you. Thousands of other families have. You can still help them live quite safely and happily in a "semi-independent" setting.

Semi-independent living situations range from ordinary apartments or condominiums intentionally set up for seniors to retirement hotels, shared housing, and continuing care communities. But before your parents enter any form of institutional housing, they may want to consider living semi-independently near you.

Part of semi-independent living is good access to transportation. Many older people are no longer safe drivers, and getting around becomes quite difficult and time-consuming. But others can drive safely well past 80 years of age. Several senior organizations provide special safe-driving courses for people over 55 or 65 years of age. The courses help people compensate for their slower reflexes and any perceptual problems they may have developed since they first learned to drive. They also teach the adverse affects of medication on driving skills and reflexes. Insurance companies often recognize the value of these programs by reducing premiums for those who pass the course. When driving skills falter, good public or para-transit can help.

In choosing a semi-independent setting, exactly how many feet or miles you interpret to be "near" is quite open, of course. The family might want your parents in another house on the same property, another apartment in the same complex, or another household in the same city. "Near" means close, but it also implies enough distance between households for everyone to maintain privacy, independence and personal space.

For the Kim family, "near" means living in the same metropolitan area. Years ago, Jordan Kim left his parents' home in New York and moved to the midwest. Now a successful attorney with a wife and three children, Jordan encouraged Dean and Gloria, his parents, to move to a nearby suburb. Although twenty miles apart, everyone in the Kim family feels much more comfortable than when Dean and Gloria lived a thousand miles away.

For the Martin family, however, "near" means within walking distance. Like many adult children, Joan Martin searched long and hard to help her parents find an apartment virtually down the street from her own home. For the Martins, living so close is great because the family can share meals, visit several times a week and take other steps to keep their lives closely intertwined.

Many families tell stories reflecting how much they enjoy the pleasures of shopping, dining out and spending weekends together. For families who are not this close-knit, having your parents live very close to you can still be appropriate when there are immediate health or money problems to worry about, or when parents need a great deal of help with everyday chores and responsibilities. When you can conveniently visit your parents without making a long trip, you find it far easier to help them keep up a satisfactory quality of life.

One of the hidden benefits of living "near" each other is that grandparents can spend more time with their grandchildren. Although many grandparents cannot handle rambunctious youngsters, in some families they become convenient and reliable babysitters. This arrangement does shift some of the burden of parenthood onto their aging shoulders, but if they are able to fulfill this responsibility, it offers significant benefits.

Grandchildren seem to thrive in the atmosphere created by loving grandparents, while grandparents tend to feel much more satisfied when they regularly spend time with their grandchildren. Be careful, though. Grandparents aren't always strong or patient enough to babysit for newborns and toddlers, who need so much attention and care. If they are capable at first, they may weaken over the years. But as the grandchildren grow toward their teenage years, the relationship seems to provide powerful, positive medicine within many families.

Elders respond well to the open warmth, boundless energy and respect they feel from very young children — even without family ties. In many European countries, and more recently in the U.S., so-called "senior/child day care centers" have begun to flourish. There are also retirement hotels and nursing homes that share facilities with child day care centers. Although the two age groups inevitably generate some friction, and some staff and administrators worry that cranky older people will curse and complain within earshot of the youngsters, the relationship generally works well.

Some family relationships, however, suffer under the strain of parents living too close. Members of one household may expect to spend more time together than those in the other household really want. Aging parents may have trouble acknowledging their adult children have other demands and responsibilities. Aging children may have difficulty balancing the time and attention they want to give their parents with the demands of their own children, their work and their daily lives. Some family members may demand too much, or expect too much accountability from others. Some will accept a plan to call at prearranged times, say once a day or three times a week. But others will call at every whim and feel rejected at the slightest inattention.

For example, Rita Johnson was uncooperative when Emily, her youngest daughter, wanted to know every time the 83-year-old woman went out. If Rita went for a walk, a drive, shopping or to a movie, Emily expected her to call before she left and after she returned. For a while, Rita tried to comply, as she had with her son Dan's intrusive behavior. But eventually, she just got angry and refused. After six months of very cold relations, Emily began to accept her parent's need for independence. Now the two are on better terms, and call each other a few times a week. Fortunately, Emily has learned not to worry every time she hears an ambulance or fire engine.

Aside from worry and unrealistic expectations, there's another danger when parents live very close. Brothers and sisters may expect the family member living nearest to their parents to shoulder extra responsibility. This can work well if everyone agrees at the outset. But if not, one or two adult children may feel some other members of the family are intentionally neglecting the parents and leaving "everything" to them, leading to family tensions.

In the Martin family, for example, Joan is happy to spend as much time as she does with her aging mother and see to her needs. She doesn't mind that her sister, Sally, visits their parents only once or twice a month — though Sally lives less than thirty minutes away. But in the Gladstone family, Betty is rapidly coming to resent that Dotty and Jack, her sister and brother, allow her to take so much of the responsibility. A heated confrontation is building up. Yet there's still time for Betty to begin openly discussing her resentment before her feelings boil over.

Here are brief discussions of some semi-independent living situations, arranged roughly in order of the least to the most services and support they generally offer:

Elder Cottages. One interesting option for semi-independent living is to install an "elder cottage" unit in your front or back yard. First popularized in Australia, full-scale elder cottages are self-contained housing units that may contain as many as 500 square feet of living space. Elder cottage units let your parents maintain much of their own lifestyle and independence while retaining the convenience and safety of living close to you. The family may find this a good compromise between having your parents live with you and having them live in a home of their own.

If you can't find or afford an elder cottage, your parents may be able to live in a mobile home, trailer, garage apartment, or some other dwelling placed near your home. Be sure to check local zoning laws.

Senior Rental Apartments are specially designed living units in the community at large that generally offer good security, ease of access and large common areas where your parents can socialize. Many senior rental apartment complexes offer an organized social program or just a spontaneous level of social activity that helps residents make friends, fight depression and stay busy.

Some also provide subsidized rents for lower-income singles or couples.

Retirement Communities have become extremely popular in the last twenty or thirty years. (These are different from "life care" communities discussed below.) Usually they are large-scale developments that become nearly self-contained neighborhoods or towns. They include rental units, single family homes and condominiums or townhouses with a clubhouse and other facilities. As a rule, retirement communities require at least one member of every household to be of a certain age, usually 55 or older.

These communities are designed to offer a range of housing prices so any qualified single or couple can find an affordable place to live. The buildings often contain broad doorways and ramps. Some communities require bathrooms to contain handrails and lowered sinks. Most retirement communities emphasize activities and social interaction with scores of clubs and hobby groups, as well as both organized and spontaneous activities that make use of the community's meeting rooms, sports facilities, health center and other common spaces. Retirement communities are often located close to shopping, medical and cultural centers, and normally provide free or low-cost transportation to popular destinations. They may have programs for providing meals and maid service to those who want them. However, retirement communities rarely provide as much care for dependent residents as do board-and-care or nursing homes. So your parents should not expect the community to provide care for them automatically. Of course, they can individually arrange for their own care by hiring attendants and so forth.

If the retirement community is organized as a cooperative, your parents buy a membership which gives them the right to occupy a particular housing unit. They don't own that particular unit, but a *share* of all units and all the common areas and facilities.

If the community is organized as a condominium, your parents can buy a particular home or apartment. They will automatically receive membership or part ownership in the association or corporation which owns the common areas and facilities.

If your parents don't want to buy a home in a retirement community, they may be able to sublet a coop or condo unit, or rent an apartment directly from the association or corporation that runs the community.

Whether it's a condo or a coop (some retirement communities contain both), one or more professional managers and paid staff usually handles most of the maintenance, gardening and security. Because the retirement community must provide the service and maintenance to keep the apartments and homes appealing and valuable, it's important the community organizations be solvent and self-supporting. You or your parents should check this before they make a financial commitment.

Most retirement communities place age restrictions on who may live there or make long-term visits to residents, so your family may face some complications if your parents die while owning a retirement community home. Your family may be able to sell or rent only to those who meet the community's standards. However, this is rarely a serious problem because of growing demand for such units.

Retirement Hotels provide another good alternative. Whether your parents are going to live within one mile or one thousand miles of your home, they may not remain healthy and independent enough to manage a full life on their own. Yet they may stay healthy enough to manage life in a "retirement hotel" for many years.

Over a million senior citizens now live in retirement hotels. They are well scattered throughout most urban and suburban neighborhoods, although you rarely notice them until you start looking. Much the same as conventional residence hotels, retirement hotels are usually modest facilities that offer a clean bedroom and living area, and one, two, or three cooked meals a day. Most retirement hotel kitchens favor basic menus, easy for older digestive systems. Residents can also participate in a broad variety of social and health maintenance programs.

Retirement hotels expect their residents to be healthy enough to move around on their own, manage their own daily care and handle themselves in day-to-day situations. Hotel managers usually don't want residents who lose bowel or bladder control, require regular medical supervision or administering of medications, are prone to wandering, or need help eating or dressing. But if a spouse moves in to provide the needed help, a debilitated parent may be able to maintain a good quality of life in a retirement hotel.

Retirement hotels can be convenient and comfortable for your parents, but the cost of renting a room can be prohibitive. Although prices vary depending on location, amenities and overall quality, in some cities it's actually cheaper — although perhaps less desirable — for your parents to take an ordinary apartment. With the monthly savings, your parents may be able to afford a maid or attendant to shop, cook and clean up after them.

Julia and Ward Matthews — a retired couple married more than fifty-five years — pay their retirement hotel about twice the cost of a nice one-bedroom apartment in the same East Coast urban neighborhood. For the extra money they get only laundry and cleaning services, and one meal a day. At this retirement hotel, as at many others all over the nation, management is heavily focused on profit. The consequences for hotel residents — as shown by the low level of service and personal care the Matthews receive — can confirm our worst expectations. But other hotels are quite acceptable for semi-active seniors.

Shared Housing (variously called "congregate housing," "shared homes," or "enriched housing") is a good choice if your parents can't manage a house, apartment or retirement hotel on their own. With shared housing, your parents move in with someone else, or have someone else move in with them. The main idea is to make a good match between living quarters and the roommates who live there. If properly set up and well supervised, shared housing can allow your parents to remain relatively independent for many more long and happy years.

Many participants in shared housing programs tend to be widows and widowers who can't afford or manage their big houses on their own. They agree to let someone else move in, share chores and help pay expenses. Aside from widows and widowers, shared households also include handicapped persons, singles and couples whose budgets are stretched very tight. If your parents live near a college, you may be able to help them find a student to rent a room and provide enough companionship and caregiving to improve their quality of life. Many older people are glad to give up a little privacy for stimulating companionship or a better place to live. Indeed, shared housing does not require a big house. Successful shared households exist in condos and small apartments.

Shared housing is so desirable and successful these days many senior centers and senior social service agencies are opening and expanding such programs. An agency running a shared-housing program tries to match up compatible combinations of both singles and couples to create new, more viable households for everyone involved.

The best shared housing agencies extensively interview hundreds of candidates and suggest matches based on everything from a person's financial resources and cooking abilities to smoking or non-smoking preferences. A good number of first-time matches don't work out. Because people can be picky and demanding, any type of shared housing can require significant compromises in eating and sleeping habits, as well as some loss of personal privacy.

If your parents want to live in shared housing, try to keep them from becoming discouraged by a bad match or two. After a few false starts, they may find a partner with whom they can share a place and call it "home" for a long time. People who are well matched often develop feelings something like family kinship — much more desirable than the formal attachments they'll likely find in most institutional settings.

Assisted Living Facilities (variously called "board-and-care homes," "residential care facilities," "sheltered housing," or "adult care homes") typically provide more services than retirement hotels or shared housing. Many provide well-balanced meals in a common dining room. Some employ staff to provide twenty-four hour care for light or infrequent personal needs.

You can think of an assisted living facility as akin to a rooming house, where homemakers maintain a family-like atmosphere for half-a-dozen or more elderly singles and couples who rent individual bedrooms in the house. These "boarders" receive all the services you'd expect in a family home — from laundry and cleaning to meals, companionship and social activities. But because they are "boarders" renting a room, they're not asked to help out with chores, as they might be in shared housing.

At some assisted living facilities, residents with mobility problems receive regular medication, special foods, diet plans and some personal care. But "heavy care" patients — who need a good deal of help eating, washing, using the bathroom and so forth — do not belong.

Assisted living facilities fall under state regulations. But state governments rarely enforce inspections and quality assurance measures for them anywhere near as stringently as they do for more institutional settings. This means assisted living facilities can be more personal, more individualized, and more responsive to the particular needs and preferences of your parents. However, it also means a particular home can violate the law, provide inferior food and even allow some of the boarders to be mistreated or abused (or murdered, as happened in one Fresno, California, board-and-care home).

To make sure your parents are treated well in an assisted living facility, you'll want to invest some time. Begin by inspecting many different homes. Look for personalities and features you think your parents will enjoy. Check the homes you favor with local authorities for any health or safety violations, such as failing to give medications on time, not feeding or keeping residents clean, inflicting bodily harm or allowing aggressive or abusive residents to hurt others. Once you select a good assisted living facility and place your parents there, visit regularly. We heard enough stories from families and from state authorities to be sure that neglected residents are frequently those without a caring family to show interest and visit. So cultivate a personal relationship with the caregivers at your parents' facility. As an added precaution, try to visit on different days of the week and at different times of the day.

Life Care (or Continuing Care Retirement) Communities offer a range of living accommodations in a single complex or location. (These are different from "retirement communities," discussed above.) At first your parents can move into an apartment and maintain a fairly independent life. As their requirements change, however, they can move to different housing units offering progressively more supervision and care as needed — through shared housing and assisted living to a nursing home. Many are operated by religious or charitable organizations. Long waiting lists or restrictions on eligibility are common. These life care communities generally require your parents to transfer all their assets to the community as payment for care for the rest of their lives. Any surplus helps pay for expansion, or for residents with fewer assets to contribute.

Your Parents Can Live in a Nursing Home

Private nursing homes can be the answer for those who are more incapacitated and dependent than residents of other housing alternatives. Even when the situation initially looks promising, however, it can be discouraging to dig deeper and discover how limited the services actually are in your town.

Because nursing homes have seen their costs increase much faster than revenues, profitability dictates the limits on quality patient care in some facilities. There are some very good nursing homes, of course. But don't assume the nearest one is good enough for your parents unless you investigate it personally and carefully. If you place your parents in a nursing home, visit regularly to check on their comfort and care. It's a good idea to plan on policing the home as long as your parents remain there.

Nursing homes are the only choice if your parents become so incapacitated they can't live independently or semi-independently in the community or with you. There are several variations on the basic idea of a nursing home, but each one is intended as a safe, fully supportive and heavily monitored residence. Nursing homes are staffed by medical professionals and attendants who give residents all the regular care and attention they need.

Nursing homes began as a place where patients could receive twenty-four hour nursing care and on-site medical emergency services at much lower cost than in a full-scale hospital. They served as a halfway house for patients newly discharged from hospitals who were still recovering from surgery or illness. Over the years, the industry has evolved to the point where recently discharged patients cannot fill all the nursing home beds. Nursing homes have adjusted to this by specializing in caregiving for older adults. Almost every nursing home now depends on this population for a large portion of its income.

These nursing homes (more professionally known as "skilled nursing" or "extended care" facilities) are rarely anyone's first choice of where to live. Countless spouses and adult children have sworn solemn oaths that: "I'll never put Mom (or Dad) away!" But moving to a nursing home is a far cry from going into cold storage. A good nursing home can represent the best choice of a place where one or both of your parents can survive comfortably and receive basic care every day.

So don't waste your breath making promises never to put your parents in a home. It's more fruitful and appropriate to promise you'll always help them choose the alternative that's *best* for them. It's a wonderful expression of your feelings for your aging parents to help them sustain the best possible quality of life — regardless of where that may be. From this perspective, helping one or both of your parents move into a nursing home (when no other choice makes as much sense) is not a death sentence, but a positive act of love.

Aside from the aversion most of us feel to the idea of an "old age home" and the potentially devastating cost, there's a much more practical worry involved in moving your parent into a nursing home. In most families, it's never easy to decide when "the time" has finally come.

Evelyn and Greg Morrison remained proud they were still vigorous and alert long after many of their friends had retired to rocking chairs. At 76 and 78 years of age, respectively, they still enjoyed travel and entertainment, and admitted they were having the best times of their long and happy lives. Their adult children, Harriet and Kevin, were equally glad to see their parents remain active and not become a burden to the family.

But then Evelyn and Greg began deteriorating rapidly. First, illness confined Evelyn to her bed for several months. Greg began showing strong mood swings and a tendency to argue with shopkeepers and acquaintances. Within a year, Harriet was so fearful of getting an emergency phone call about her parents she couldn't fall asleep at night. To prevent problems, her brother Kevin began taking control of their parents' financial affairs and Harriet got in the habit of dropping by the apartment about once a week. Late one afternoon she found them in bed, weak and hungry, with no money in the house and no food in the refrigerator. After that, Harriet and Kevin began visiting much more.

Over the next several months, Evelyn began to lose bladder and bowel control. One day, Greg went wandering away and could not be found for six hours. Harriet and Kevin tried to solve these problems and provide their parents with the care and supervision they needed. They worked and worried themselves nearly to the point of exhaustion before a case manager finally convinced them Evelyn and Greg should long since have moved to a nursing home. Within a month of finding a good nursing home for their parents, Harriet and Kevin regained their health and most of their happiness. They felt very secure in the knowledge their parents were well cared for between visits.

Every family is different, of course. But if your parents give you a strong and definite signal that they're candidates for a nursing home, you'll be in rare company. Most times, parents decline so slowly that family members barely notice when they first lose the ability to live safely and comfortably on their own. In the Granger family, adult sons and daughters living near their parents kept reporting that Dan, the 83 year-old autocrat of the family, was stable and doing well. "He's still sharp," Zack told his brother, Phil, who lived a thousand miles away. But when Phil and his wife came for a visit, they found Dan somewhat disoriented and showing distinct signs of forgetfulness. Phil pointed this out to his brother and his mother, Estelle, but they insisted he was mistaken. At a family picnic a week later, the family noticed Dan asking the same questions over and over, and had to admit he was no longer as "sharp" as he had been. Dan continued to get worse for another year, until he was so severely incapacitated he could survive only in a local nursing home.

One rule of thumb for deciding when your parents should go to a nursing home is the "it hurts me more than it helps you" guideline. In many families, there comes a time when the effort needed to care adequately for parents or an aging spouse no longer delivers a big improvement in quality of life, yet the emotional rabbit-punches the caregiver is absorbing threaten his or her own health, or threaten to destroy family life for spouses, brothers, sisters, children, or grandchildren. Sometimes, putting Mom or Dad into a nursing home doesn't provide much better care for her or him. But it leads to a world of improvement for the caregiver at home.

Evaluating Nursing Homes

All nursing homes are not equally pleasant and well managed. At first, the differences may be subtle and hard to see. But as you look more carefully, you'll begin to notice small things that can make a world of difference when your parent becomes confined there. Before anyone in the family signs a contract or brings in Mom or Dad to stay, make a careful evaluation of the home, including its facilities, staff, basic services, programs, cost and amenities.

To begin evaluating a nursing home, talk with local social workers who specialize in such matters, as well as hospital discharge planners, private case managers, clergy and friends. Professionally, some of the experts probably won't say anything too critical about particular nursing homes. But privately, they may share with you the "generally accepted" opinions that circulate among the professionals who work in and around the nursing homes every day.

Visit the highly recommended homes. (You may also want to visit one of the "unrecommended" homes to help you recognize and appreciate the differences.) Make an appointment to discuss your parent's needs with the nursing home administrator, social service director, or admissions manager. But also be canny and make a separate, unannounced visit during weekend or evening hours.

Both the nursing home and its administrator should be fully licensed by the appropriate state agency. The medical director should be fully qualified, licensed and readily available to residents. If you're expecting government or private insurance to pick up some of the cost of living in the nursing home, make sure the facility is duly certified and compliant with all applicable regulations. Look for a full set of handrails, smoke detectors, fire alarms, clearly marked and unobstructed exits, and obvious freedom from fire hazards. Observe bedrooms to see if they have both outside windows and hallway access, and check the toilets for wheelchair access.

Talk with various staff people and award points for how helpful, friendly and concerned they seem in regard to the residents. See how quickly they respond to call bells. No nursing home is as pleasant as your parent's own home, obviously. Nevertheless you can and should pay attention to your own judgments about the differences in quality among various nursing homes you are considering. After a few visits, you'll notice a lot more than you saw at first.

As you walk the hallways and peer into the common rooms, pay attention to how content and well-cared-for the residents appear, how pleasant and comfortable the whole environment seems. You can feel good about a nursing home that has its residents clean, dressed appropriately for their activities and interacting as much as possible with each other. You should be concerned if patients seem over-medicated.

Study any bulletin boards in the home for notices about the activity and entertainment schedules, as well as any special programs that take place there. Peek in on a few of the activity sessions to see how staff and residents interact. You'll want to place your parent in a home where people working at every level will take time to talk with Mom or Dad and will show a personal interest.

Make sure the interior of the home is clean, warm, bright and pleasing to the senses, with wide, unobstructed hallways. The dining room and common areas for activities should be neat and attractive. Avoid nursing homes with strong odors of medication or disinfectants. Heavy scents can mask less desirable smells underneath. Look for safe, well-lit exteriors, with an outside lawn or terrace residents can easily reach to enjoy sun and fresh air.

The kitchen should be set up with food preparation areas widely separated from garbage and dishwashing areas, and there should be enough refrigeration for all perishables. The food service director should seem knowledgeable, and interested in your parent's appetites and eating habits.

Before your family chooses a particular nursing home, consider its location. Family and friends will visit more at a home conveniently located and easily accessible. For your parent who lives there, you'll want the home to be safe and relatively quiet.

In addition to your family's opinions, there are "official" opinions available about nursing homes. State agencies survey and visit licensed nursing homes at least once a year. Their reports are public information and may be openly posted in the home, along with violations of regulations and complaints from residents and their families. Ask to see the last two or three state audits or evaluation reports. Look them over. You'll probably be shocked at the sheer number of violations and complaints, even in the best nursing homes. But a long list doesn't always signal a bad nursing home. Some violations are minor and easily fixed.

If you study the violations at several nursing homes, you'll begin to notice differences in the number and severity of significant problems, such as infestations, unsafe practices and neglect of helpless residents. The real tip-offs to an undesirable nursing home are when the same major violation appears on two or more state reports and when you see no sign of improvement or effort to improve.

No matter how bleak things may seem, try to avoid feeling discouraged. As you'll discover, nursing home problems tend to come and go in waves. A new administrator can make significant overall changes in a previously unsatisfactory facility. Just as important, a different nursing supervisor or aide assigned to your parent can instantly bring major improvements to his or her daily quality of life. On the other hand, a good facility can rapidly go downhill when staff or administrators change, so don't become complacent about a nursing home you feel is satisfactory.

Life in a Nursing Home

Despite what you and your parents may have heard, nursing homes are far from the inevitable dead ends many people imagine. Many people enter nursing homes to convalesce or recuperate after a hospitalization, and go home after six months of care, or less. The typical long-term nursing home resident lives for six to ten years after moving in. For some, the nursing home functions much like a shared apartment or residential hotel — but with far less demanded of them. Although nursing homes typically hold several hundred residents, they try hard to provide individualized care. Most good nursing homes can prepare residents their own carefully planned and well balanced diets, served the way they like it. Nurses and aides learn each patient's needs, wants and likes, and try to provide each with as much or as little assistance and personal care as seems right.

The best nursing homes offer their residents a wide range of services and special programs. In addition to administrators and clerks, medical director, nurses and daily care aides, nursing homes often employ specially trained therapists, activities coordinators, social service specialists, a food service director or dietician and religious staff. Most quality nursing homes benefit from a host of community volunteers who regularly offer their time or special skills, or who tend to religious concerns.

All this care can be expensive. Within a broad range, the cost of living in an average nursing home for a year is about the same as a nurse's annual salary. It's almost as if your parent is paying for a full-time personal attendant. In reality, of course, residents get part-time services from a half-dozen or more professionals and aides, as well as their room and board. Obviously, the cost of living in a nursing home can quickly drain a family's financial resources. Most families use personal funds to start their aging parent in a nursing home, and are surprised to find that private insurance does not cover long-term care. Sooner or later, the family depletes its financial resources and falls back on government insurance. Make sure your parents select a nursing home that accepts this government insurance. Otherwise, the administrator may decide to transfer your parent elsewhere as soon as private insurance and personal funds can no longer pay the monthly bill. Also, see if the home provides the same or nearly the same services to both private pay and government pay residents. If there's a significant difference, your parent may suffer a major setback in quality of life when family finances run low.

Improving Quality of Life for Nursing Home Residents

Your parent can get more satisfaction from life in a good nursing home than from an inadequately supported life in the community. Occasionally, husbands and wives live together in a nursing home and maintain an enjoyable relationship. Evelyn and Greg Morrison were able to move to a nursing home together as a couple and continue their married life. Other families tell stories of elderly parents who met someone in a nursing home, then married and lived there as a couple far happier than before.

However, the vast majority of nursing home residents are forced to move in because at home they simply cannot receive all the help they need. They may be widowed, or too disabled or ill for a spouse to look after adequately. That's why nursing homes are witness to visiting spouses who sit for hours talking with their long-time companions.

Family visits do more than "cheer up" the parent in the nursing home. Visits help family members feel more comfortable with the inevitable end of life. They provide a chance to clear away old business and build up an emotional reservoir that will help assuage the coming grief. Frequent visits can also help your parent maintain a better quality of life in the nursing home. You can easily bring a favorite food or a new hat, for example. One trick Estelle Granger learned is to keep a candy dish filled in Dan's nursing home room. She let the staff know it was for them. Coming in to get a hard candy or mint, aides and nurses naturally saw to Dan Granger's needs and kept him more comfortable.

Another payoff from family visits is that they tell the staff you're interested and you're monitoring your parent's quality of life and daily treatment. Under present regulations, nursing homes must keep extensive medical records on every patient, and you are free to examine your parent's whenever you wish. Check these records on some of your visits. Notice whether a physician regularly visits Mom or Dad, and whether too much medication is creating lethargy or depression. Some nursing homes rely at least partly on drugs to keep patients quiet. The Resource Guide in the back of this book has a list of some drugs to watch for carefully.

Many nursing homes are open to visits from family and friends at least twelve to sixteen hours a day, seven days a week. Spouses generally want to visit more than adult children or grandchildren, but few spouses come every day. There are no hard and fast rules for visiting. It's best to establish what you feel to be a reasonable visiting pattern, then stick to it. If your parent recognizes family members and converses well, you might want to visit more often. If Alzheimer's Disease or other senility prevents Mom or Dad from recognizing family members, you may want to visit less frequently. You may want to bring your parent home for birthdays or other happy occasions, or you may prefer to do all your visiting in the nursing home. Once you establish a pattern that fits in with the other demands on your life, don't torture yourself for not going more often.

In fact, your visits are only one contribution to your parent's quality of life. You can involve yourself in the daily life of the home. You can also join one of the "family and friends" groups that most nursing homes support. These groups meet regularly and talk about the problems, feelings and practical considerations of having a close relative or loved one living there. These sessions can provide important help in coping with the emotional burdens of parenting your aging parents. Additionally, most good nursing homes have active "residents' councils" with a quasi-official status; the administrator relies on its members for ideas and special efforts to resolve problems and to help develop better nursing home policies and activities.

A bolder approach may be for you to become a "volunteer ombudsman." In many states, people who qualify for this position gain real authority and responsibility. The ombudsman is asked to monitor the level of care at area nursing homes and then regularly report on conditions to local health officials. It's a part-time job, but requires a steady commitment. Once your parent moves to a nursing home, however, there's probably no better position from which to make sure he or she gets the best possible care!

There are several other ways family members can improve the quality of life for parents forced out of their own homes and relegated to institutional settings. The methods work for any type of institutional or group residence facility.

Learn the schedule: Encourage your parents to develop a daily routine that fits the patterns and schedules of the new residence. Then learn it and follow it yourself. Rather than ask Mom or Dad to leave a movie or a bingo game half finished just because you arrive for a visit, show up during times you know are free. Members of the Granger family try not to arrive during Dan's naps or therapy sessions, but they often show up in time to share a meal with him. Indeed, Zack and his wife made it a point to join Dan for a midday or evening meal each day during his first week in the nursing home. Later, they timed some of their visits to coincide with his free periods in the afternoon or on weekends. If you have the flexibility in your own life, you can help your parent adjust and work into a comfortable daily routine by spending time with him or her on the new schedule.

Share activities: A good way to spend quality time with your parent is to share some enjoyable activity. You may want to help with writing a letter to a relative or friend. You may enjoy reading a book out loud, playing cards, looking at a photo album, or working together on a puzzle. If your parent is able, you may want to go outside together, visit a nearby store, have a meal in a restaurant, or simply sit and enjoy the weather.

Another very interesting and informative activity can be to create an "oral history." Simply ask your parent to tell stories they remember of their own past, and of their parents and their grandparents. To record their memories, all you need do is set up a tape machine. If they ramble or run out of stories, ask them questions. In too many families, virtually all of this history is lost forever. But you can preserve it. Few parents are cooperative in starting oral histories, but you may later find it was worth the extra effort to convince them and persist in the project. Just five or ten minutes a day saved on tape can add up to a major, lifelong legacy for the rest of the family. In addition, the process of recording an oral history can help keep your parent better oriented and alert.

Treat the place as a residence: Although many facilities look like hospitals, people live there, and many will never move out. Try to behave as though you were a guest in an ordinary home. Help your parent personalize the room as much as possible with family photographs, plants and favorite objects. Even if you visit regularly, send greeting cards on birthdays, holidays and at random. Display the most recent pictures drawn by their grandchildren or great-grandchildren. Bring flowers from your garden, or special home-made or home-grown foods they enjoy. Make yourself comfortable in your parent's room and in the common areas, but be wary of invading others' private spaces. Get to know the staff. In a sense, they "live" there, too. Treat each of them warmly and they may return some of that warmth to your parent when you are not around.

Touch Your Parent: Confined parents will enjoy some physical contact with you and other family members. It feels comforting and pleasurable when you place your hand gently on an arm or shoulder during a conversation, or brush their hair. Some adult children like to give their parents an occasional manicure or a massage.

Engage in lively conversations: When you visit, talk with your parents about your day. Ask about theirs. Discuss the weather, business and current events, and plan your next visit. Listen to your parent and ask questions. Most important, bring Mom or Dad up to date about the rest of the family: what people are doing, how fast the children are growing, who's having a birthday or a new baby or getting a promotion, and so forth. These ordinary items of information may seem out of place to you in a residence facility, but this "normalcy" is extremely helpful in maintaining Mom or Dad's sense of family membership, personal identity, self-esteem and orientation to reality.

Monitor and respond to complaints: Many conversations may revolve around your parent's irritations and adjustment problems. For example, some parents complain loudly and often about how others treat them. Naturally, you'll want to investigate and make sure Mom or Dad is getting the best possible care and not being mistreated in any way.

If you find a complaint to be valid, take steps to remedy it immediately. Use the proper channels to bring the problem to staff and supervisors without delay. Be polite but firm. If you remain unsatisfied, or your parent is subject to abusive or neglectful treatment, consider moving Mom or Dad directly to another nursing home, or into your own home while you look for a better place.

On the other hand, you may be surprised to find your parent's complaints have little basis in fact or reasonableness. For instance, Dan Granger frequently complained he was not being fed. Depressed parents often complain of harassment. Checking further, you're likely to find —

as the Granger family did — your parent eats heartily at every meal, or that "harassment" comes from attendants trying only to lighten your parent's depression. In many families, complaining is a common way for parents to make a stronger bid for attention. Unfounded and repetitive complaints are often the only way your parent can convey the message: "You're neglecting me by leaving me here against my wishes!"

Should you find your parent's complaints unwarranted, remain sensitive and supportive. Continue to listen to the complaints. Make it a point of pride not to become irritated or angry. Do whatever you can to make your parent's daily life a little better, but understand you cannot make life perfect for anyone, and that Mom or Dad may not be able to recognize the improvements you do provide.

Adjustment Problems for the Nursing Home Resident

Placing your parent in a nursing home can cause you pain and suffering, but your parents are more directly impacted by the move than you are. In most cases, adjusting to nursing home life (and to living apart) is extremely frightening for them.

Although the move to a nursing home usually improves parents' health and safety, it is an undeniably institutional environment. It is only normal for Mom or Dad to miss some of the personal touches, the family interactions and the enjoyments of living more independently at home.

Anyone confined to a nursing home suffers both a real and a perceived loss of independence and privacy. Mom and Dad remember living on their own, but are now part of a large "community" with hundreds of residents, where each person gives up at least some control over his or her personal time, meals, and overall freedom to pursue favorite activities. People down the hall or across the room may blast a radio or TV, may rudely demand help in making telephone calls or moving around the facility, may want to talk without wanting to listen, or may complain loudly when others exhibit some of this same behavior.

Your parent also stands at least some chance of reacting to the move with a fairly rapid loss of self-esteem. Greg Morrison was typical of many nursing home residents who quickly lose much of their sense of competence and mastery over their world. In addition to his own loss of control and independence, he was under stress simply from seeing the physical and mental conditions of the other residents — some of whom seemed barely alive — and from living in confinement with these patients' noises, complaints, unpleasant habits and accidents.

Your parent can begin to feel almost totally helpless in the nursing home and therefore less lovable than when he or she lived more independently. As you can probably imagine, it's very unpleasant to feel that your family has consigned you to "an old age home" — especially if it happens against your wishes. Even if Mom or Dad realizes he or she is seriously ill, it's entirely understandable for your parent to suffer at least some damaged feelings.

In addition, the simple fact of suddenly being separated from the family and sleeping in a new environment creates a lot of stress in most people, at least during an initial adjustment period. Such abrupt transitions may also create a domino effect of other problems. In other words, once your parent moves to a nursing home, he or she might deteriorate even further very quickly. Some parents seem never to adjust completely to life in a nursing home. They appear to suffer for a while and then pass away.

Others will live for years and years in a nursing home with only a thin connection to their former life. But most — like Evelyn and Greg Morrison — make a full or nearly full adjustment after a few weeks or months. Although many nursing home residents frequently ask to "come home" again, at some level they can almost always understand their own helplessness and the inability of the family to care for them.

Adjustment Problems for the Family

For the parent who remains at home, adjustments can be extremely painful. Placing one parent in a nursing home means the other is relieved of most caregiving responsibilities and provides some freedom. But the daily schedule may now seem empty. There may be no one to cook for, no one to consider in making plans, and no live-in companionship. Mom or Dad may also feel some guilt over confining their spouse to a nursing home. They may overlook how much this change improves the situation for the whole family.

Adult children also face adjustment problems after one of their parents moves to a nursing home. Some adult children are more apprehensive about nursing homes than their parents. You may feel you could have done more to take care of your aging parent, or that you could have picked a better nursing home. You may dislike the tedium and inconvenience of visits, as well as the sights, sounds and smells you may find inside the place.

As Harriet and Kevin (Morrison) learned, however, the benefits of a nursing home often provide such a quick quality-of-life improvement for those who previously carried the caregiving burden that positive emotional adjustments can follow fairly quickly. As we have described, both Harriet and Kevin became exhausted and overwrought by pressures of caring for their aging parents. Both felt relieved when Evelyn and Greg went to a nursing home, and with their caregiving burdens much lightened they enjoyed their extra time alone with their spouses and children.

Despite the improvement that may follow, the rest of the family may never adequately resolve the issue of "putting Mom or Dad away." However, when the family has tried hard to keep the parent at home and has found this unworkable or dangerous — as the Grangers did — most family members usually adjust more easily. They will also find in their hearts a little more tolerance and sympathy for the parent's emotional distress at being left alone and confined.

CHAPTER 3

FINANCES

Helping your parents handle their finances can be one of the most important areas in which you provide assistance. This can include monitoring and managing their cash, income and other assets, as well as helping them select and purchase insurance, manage their tax obligations, handle credit, obtain public benefits and safeguard other aspects of their financial well-being.

Your parents' savings and other assets represent the fruits of their lifetime labor. Running short of money, now or in the future, will significantly narrow their options. Financial losses can hurt their self-confidence and ruin their enjoyment of life. Preserving their assets helps assure their self-esteem as well as their financial freedom.

Getting Started

Chances are your parents have a significant amount of money and other assets well worth protecting and managing. Four out of five older Americans have a nest egg to help pay for their last years, and people over 65 own assets worth about $8 trillion! If your family is lucky, your parents will have enough money to live comfortably for many years to come, and they'll retain their health and mental faculties well enough to manage their own finances.

However, some families are far less fortunate. In about ten percent of American families, the elderly parents can barely make ends meet, while in others, they have lost the ability to manage their funds. The Williams have minimal income and assets. They survive by living with their adult daughter Greta, and by letting their son-in-law, Bill, handle their money more carefully than they could do by themselves. Willa Gladstone has enough money to keep herself comfortable, but can no longer manage it properly. Left to herself, she might not pay all her bills, she might waste her money or be victimized by con artists.

It's a good idea to talk with your parents about their finances as soon as possible, even if it seems they'll never need your help. You may feel financial planning is a low priority right now. But you'd be wrong. Many financial arrangements take weeks, months, or even years to begin working favorably. You must recognize your obligations and goals, research your opportunities, think about your options and plan your steps. Then allow additional time to begin carrying out your plans and for them to bear fruit.

If you wait for a crisis to develop, you may have trouble obtaining all the information or legal authority you need in time to do the best job for them. You may overlook some available options and feel uncertain about what your parents really want. Furthermore, your judgment may not be as calm and steady as it should be when making financial decisions.

The better approach is to get things set up now, before your parents suffer an accident or illness, or face the onset of other problems. This way, assets will be properly invested and financial mechanisms will be in place early enough to provide significant help when needed.

This type of advance financial management is often called "retirement planning." Most older Americans are aware of the need for some type of "estate planning," such as wills, gifts and trusts. Unfortunately, they rarely give as much attention to the more complex area of "retirement planning," which must take into account the changing consequences of many different financial decisions and activities during all of their remaining years.

Too frequently, older Americans simply outlive their financial plans. This problem arises because actuaries can predict only *how many people* per 100,000 will die in a given year; they can't tell you *which ones*. What's more, no one can predict how healthy your aging Mom or Dad will remain in their last years. If your parents don't have a suitable retirement plan, they are risking their financial security on worse odds than the weakest junk bond ever offered. Unintentionally, your parents could become what they least desire to be: "A burden to their children."

Even if your parents are still working full time, it's not too early to discuss how their financial situation may change as they grow older. Retirement planning involves calculating expenditures and anticipating investment and other income, then balancing these figures to fund a sustainable and satisfactory lifestyle.

Many families develop a plan on their own, combining current financial planning with long-term retirement planning. However, you may want your parents to seek advice from independent retirement planners, or from experts who work for unions, banks, investment houses, or accounting firms. Be cautious in accepting any advice, though. Some financial planners are little more than glorified sales people, and many earn commissions based on the investment products — annuities, bonds and so forth — their clients purchase. The most reliable information comes from advisors who have no stake in how your parents actually invest.

Coping With Complexity and Danger

Today's financial system is more complex than ever before, so it is increasingly common for parents to make mistakes in choosing where to place their retirement nest egg. The tough financial questions begin with: Where should they keep their money? What insurance and other services should they purchase? How much can they afford to pay for living expenses without depleting their financial reserves? There are dozens of other concerns, depending on your parents' specific financial resources and obligations. They'll almost certainly need advice in choosing the best financial strategies and tactics, and may require help in putting those choices into effect.

One big danger is inflation. It can eat away at your parents' financial assets even while it increases their living expenses. As a result, more and more aging parents face a financial shortfall. Too often, aging parents understandably fear a major shortage of money. They can't afford to live as comfortably as they would like, and must make some cutbacks to avoid a financial crisis in the very near future.

Other major drains on your parents' financial resources can result from medical care, personal services, or nursing care needed to battle chronic illness, disability, or mental deterioration. If your parents' health begins to fail, these costs can add up alarmingly fast. Without the proper insurance and knowledge of how to handle these expenses, your parents can quickly deplete their financial reserves.

Fortunately, most elderly Americans can receive some form of financial help from government sources, most commonly medical coverage, veteran's and Social Security benefits and other publicly supported income or services. However, these benefits don't always flow freely. You must be alert to all available resources and know how to help your parents obtain all their entitlements.

Investment of your parents' assets is one of the most important aspects of any financial management program. A basic investment rule to observe during or just before retirement is this: **Do not take chances with more than five percent of the total nest egg.** It's foolhardy to allow any possibility that too much of your parents' hard-earned capital might be lost to them forever. If money is lost in one investment, your parents' other investments simply won't have much time in which to grow and replace it. Also, any loss of capital can immediately reduce your parents' income and force cutbacks in their lifestyle.

If your parents observe this five percent rule, they will have to rely mainly on stable, safe investments like bonds, CDs and money market vehicles. They will have to favor investments backed by government guarantees or private insurance. Because these are very safe, they pay relatively low interest returns. Higher-paying investments may look more attractive, but they always entail higher risk.

By favoring safe investments, your parents will receive a fairly fixed income from their retirement funds (which may be invested through Independent Retirement Accounts, Simplified Employee Pension Plans, job-related retirement plans and more). Social Security provides another fixed source of income. Because they have little chance to increase their income significantly, your parents will want to focus on managing their life-style to fit their known income and assets.

A good way to do this is to help your parents write down a series of financial goals. These goals should in-clude at least a monthly or annual target "income" from all sources, adjusted to reflect the likely tax bill on that income. They may also include one-year and five-year targets for their total net worth. With goals established, you can help your parents begin to formulate a budget and some prudent financial strategies.

Taking Control

Taking control of any aspect of your parents' lives is a serious responsibility. You'll want to be even more careful than you are with your own money, if only to prevent any legal or emotional fallout from your actions.

If you're going to help your parents manage their finances, you'll need a complete listing of all their assets. This should include:

- Bank accounts, certificates of deposit, safe deposit boxes and their contents.

- Itemized lists of stocks, bonds and mutual funds (with all relevant account and certificate numbers).

- Descriptions of all personal property, with addresses and details of any real estate your parents may own, including burial plots.

- Policy numbers for all life and health insurance, with premium due dates, current cash values (if any), benefit amounts, specific coverages and exclusions.

It's also important to have a record of your parents' financial liabilities, including both long- and short-term debts on everything from cars and houses to outstanding credit card charges and personal loans.

All this information collected in one place is called a "balance sheet," and makes the best starting point for sound financial management. It shows the total value of all your parents assets, their "net worth" at the time. The next step is to calculate income and expenses. From there, it's easy to build a monthly budget.

This budget should include (but not be limited to): rent or mortgage; fire, theft and liability insurance; utilities; an anticipated amount for home repairs and improvements; income and real estate taxes; groceries and other food expenses; household expenses, perhaps including cleaning, gardening, or other paid help; car expenses, including repairs, insurance, and fuel; life insurance, if needed; medical insurance, routine doctors' bills, prescriptions, and other health care expenses; clothing; grooming, such as a hairdresser or barber; incidentals; and entertainment.

While you're considering the practical aspects of helping your parents run their lives, make sure you know all the details: where they keep important papers like life insurance policies and stock certificates; and the names of their doctors, financial advisors and clergy.

Voluntary Financial Management

Mildred and Addison Williams were able to recognize his inability to fully manage their affairs, and were happy to let their son-in-law, Bill, take over. A voluntary financial management agreement such as this between the parents and one or more adult children is an easy and efficient way to hand over some or all of the responsibility for managing the money. Because the arrangement is voluntary, your parents can still act on their own behalf any time they wish. Naturally, whoever assumes control should consult your parents before taking any action on important matters.

There are several different ways you or another family member can assume voluntary control of your parents' finances:

Power of Attorney

Your parents can sign special documents that give you — or anyone they designate — the legal right to act on their behalf. This power of attorney makes you the "attorney in fact" for your parent and gives you wide authority to cash their checks, pay their bills, and otherwise spend, save and transfer their money. You can add your name to their safe deposit boxes and bank accounts, and sign contracts — such as apartment leases — which are binding upon them. In short, you can do virtually everything necessary to handle their affairs.

The power of attorney each parent signs should be both **broad** and **durable**. That is, the wording should be "broad" enough to include the power to borrow, give and purchase; to file tax forms; to execute trusts; and to allow you a considerable range of action and authority, instead of a narrow list of duties. In addition, it should have the proper wording to be "durable" under the state laws where your parent resides, letting you continue as "attorney in fact" *after* your parent becomes unable to act for him- or herself, whether through accident, illness, or old age. (Better stationery stores generally carry standardized forms which each parent can fill in to grant durable powers of attorney.)

A power of attorney may expire unless your parent renews it regularly. Mom or Dad can, of course, revoke it any time they wish, and it automatically ends when the grantor dies. Since you needn't exercise a power of attorney, you can — and probably should — encourage your parents to sign these documents well before they would want you to take control. You can store the documents safely until you actually need to exercise some of the powers your parents have given you. It may be best for each power of attorney to designate two or three people; if one becomes incapacitated, another can step forward to take charge of your parent's affairs.

If your parents are reluctant to grant power of attorney while they can still act on their own behalf, they may want to utilize a special "springing" form of this document available in quite a few states. A springing power of attorney becomes operative only when a specified event occurs, such as mental incompetence. Again, your parents can revoke this springing power of attorney at any time. In the event of a sudden calamity, however, they can be protected by someone they know and trust.

Joint Ownership

Another voluntary way to handle your parents' financial affairs is to become a joint owner of their checking account, savings account, home and other assets. As a legal owner, you need no special documents or court orders to exercise control. Once you become a joint owner of your parents' savings account, for example, you can withdraw money to pay their medical bills, rent and other expenses. Another potential advantage of joint ownership is that, upon the death of your parent, you automatically inherit the assets.

But there are drawbacks to joint ownership. For example, under joint ownership the "basis" (or original value of the asset for tax purposes) does not change when the original owner dies. Thus, a house purchased for $50,000, transferred to joint ownership with a son or daughter, and sold immediately after the death of the parent for $150,000 would yield a $100,000 profit subject to income taxes. The same house *not* transferred to joint ownership, but bequeathed to the son or daughter, would acquire the higher basis and thus allow all profit on the sale to escape income tax. Also, joint ownership grants each party total ownership of some assets, so any joint owner of a bank account could withdraw all the money and leave the other joint owners with nothing. However, one joint owner of a home or car cannot sell it without getting the signatures of all other joint owners.

Trust Agreements

A trust is a legal arrangement that gives control over specific assets to a person or an institution (called the trustee), often with implications for the taxes levied on the entrusted assets. There are many different types of trusts your parents can establish. Mildred and Addison Williams, for example, found it advisable to establish a *living trust* with themselves, as well as Greta and her husband, Bill, designated as trustees. This gives Bill easy control over the assets and provides a good way of insulating the Williams' small estate from probate costs.

Trust laws are highly complex and detailed, and a small mistake in the paperwork can invalidate an entire trust arrangement. If your parents decide to use a trust, it's wise to work with a trust attorney or the trust department of a bank or other financial institution. These specialists can help you and your parents determine which trust is right for them, and can often handle the legal work to get that trust established.

Representative Payee

This is a person your parent or the Social Security Administration appoints to receive your parent's Social Security or Veterans Administration payments. The representative payee receives the benefit checks and becomes legally responsible for using the money to help pay your parent's expenses. Under Social Security guidelines, a representative payee must first use all Social Security benefits for your parent's food, shelter and daily basic needs. If any money is left over, it's OK to use it to help support your parent's legal dependents.

As a Representative Payee, be particularly careful not to mingle any of your parent's benefits with your own money. Maintain separate accounts, or at least complete records to show you saved or prudently invested any surplus on your parent's behalf. If you misuse the funds, you'll not only have to repay them to your parent, you'll face fines and imprisonment.

Asset Transfer in Return for Lifetime Benefits

This is a sophisticated legal arrangement in which a person voluntarily deeds away an asset in return for a benefit to be received for the rest of his or her life. Some parents use this to give their children the family home in return for lifelong care. However, the arrangement is most often used when there are few or no immediate family members to help care for an aging couple or individual. People tend to give large assets (such as their entire estate, or a house and furnishings) to institutions (such as a life-care community or a university) in return for a lifetime benefit (and sometimes tax advantages). In the case of a life-care community, the benefit would be a promise of free lifetime room, board and medical care; in the case of a university, it might be the lifetime right to live in the home, rent free, while taking current tax deductions for the donation. Many life-care communities rely on signing dozens of contracts like this to meet their annual operating budgets. This arrangement can work well for all those involved.

The danger, of course, is that the recipient of the asset can declare bankruptcy and escape any legal obligation to provide the promised benefit. Even when the recipient breaks the promise, the court may uphold the original transfer of the asset — removing it from the family forever. Obviously, your parents — and anyone — must be extremely cautious in signing any asset transfer.

Involuntary Financial Management and Guardianship

Most families prefer a voluntary arrangement over an involuntary one because it provides more flexibility and eliminates the costly legal process needed to take financial control against someone's wishes or after incompetence is established. In some families, however, there are too many obstacles to voluntary transfer of financial control. Most often, the parents either don't recognize the need for help from their children, or actively resist any notion of giving up control. When parents can no longer fend for themselves and have not made any legal arrangements for voluntary transfer of financial control, family members must seek an involuntary financial management arrangement.

Although laws vary from state to state, in general it takes a court order to transfer assets away from a parent who is no longer mentally competent. The court must be petitioned to study your parent and determine competence. The court will usually evaluate whether your parent can sensibly manage his or her property, is likely to fall prey to unscrupulous individuals, or lacks the capacity to make other important decisions.

If the court judges your parent to be incompetent, it appoints a guardian or conservator — sometimes a spouse, daughter, or son. But a guardian or conservator need not be one of the family. Courts often presume family members to be financially unsophisticated. They prefer to appoint guardians and conservators from the ranks of bank trust departments, lawyers, accountants, or other disinterested parties with solid financial management credentials. Once appointed, the guardian or conservator is entitled to receive fees for all services and expenses, paid by the estate.

Sometimes this is the best available alternative, but guardianship and conservatorship can be a very undesirable condition. The court generally strips your parent of all or most legal rights. Mom or Dad becomes almost an "object" totally under someone else's control. The whole legal process is also expensive, draining resources from your parent's nest egg without directly improving his or her quality of life.

Building a Monthly Budget

A monthly budget is one of the basic tools of financial planning. Your parents' budget should list all their present and anticipated expenses, as well as all their sources of income. Your parents can look back at past checkbooks to see how much money they spend on various items. For income, they can consider savings, stocks, bonds and other investments, as well as property which

they can live in, use, or rent out to others. If an asset —
like original art, collectible items and antiques — doesn't
generate income, they can consider selling it (at a fair
price, rather than a big discount) and investing or spending the cash to beef up their monthly income.

It's best to be very conservative about including
anticipated but unproven sources of income. That is, your
parents may be able to safely count on making a small
amount from a business or profession they know, but
would be unwise to expect a large amount of income from
an entirely new second career. Similarly, in a given economic climate they may safely count on receiving six or
eight percent interest on their savings and other investments, but not twelve or fifteen percent.

With a completed budget in hand, you can help your
parents begin to estimate how well their available assets
will support the lifestyle they desire. At this stage, you
can also begin to look for areas in which to make any
necessary adjustments to bring income and expenses into
line.

Social Security and Other Government Benefits

Despite what you may think, Social Security benefits
were never intended to support anyone in retirement.
Congress designed them as a public supplement to a
person's private retirement income. Although no one gets
rich on Social Security, these checks can help your aging
parents live more comfortably.

Unfortunately, a considerable number of people
eligible for financial assistance are not receiving everything to which they are entitled. The most common reason
is simply not knowing about and applying for various
programs. Check up on your parents' total eligibility and

make sure they receive all government benefits to which they are entitled.

The Social Security Administration will go through your parents' records and provide both a *total of their earnings* and an *estimate of their benefits*. If the total lifetime earnings acknowledged by Social Security seem different from the income your parents actually earned, they may be short-changed on their benefits. Your parents can appeal the discrepancy by showing Social Security proof of their earnings. If Social Security's estimate of the benefits your parents should be receiving is significantly higher than what they are actually receiving, they may not be receiving their full entitlement.

There's also a valuable program called Supplementary Security Income (SSI) providing disability benefits to needy individuals 65 and over, and to those who are blind or otherwise disabled. SSI income standards are fairly low, so that in many cases those already receiving Social Security have too much income to be eligible. However, it's important for disabled persons to apply for SSI anyway, not only because they may qualify, but because they may find themselves eligible for related Medicaid and state programs worth more than SSI itself.

Other government benefits programs include Food Stamps to help families pay for nutritious foods, and Low Income Energy Assistance to help cover the cost of utilities for lights, heat and cooking. Again, for each program your parents must apply and meet certain eligibility requirements. If they qualify, however, the government effectively boosts their income every year by hundreds or thousands of dollars.

Pensions and Retirement Accounts

If either of your parents worked for a company with a pension plan, they should follow virtually the same procedures as with Social Security. Encourage them to call the pension office to obtain a record of their earnings and an estimate of their expected pension benefits. If you find any discrepancies, take steps to correct them before your parents are hurt by loss of pension income.

Your parents may also have private retirement accounts earning regular income. Your parents have the choice of taking this retirement money in a lump sum or in regular payments over a period of years based on life expectancies. If they've already chosen one option and want to change their mind, the IRS offers procedures to do so. Since the tax rules establishing minimum and maximum distributions from retirement accounts and pension plans are complicated, your parents should always consult a tax advisor or check with the IRS before taking any action.

Retirement plans may provide only a portion of your parents' income. They may have savings, or own stocks, bonds and other assets which either produce income or which they can sell for money to live on.

Savings Accounts

Savings pay interest your parents can use to cover monthly expenses. Rather than place all their savings in an account paying only about five percent, your parents can keep the bulk of their savings in "tiers" of higher-paying accounts.

The basic idea is to keep only enough money to cover day-to-day expenses in a low interest account, and back this up with enough for three to six months in a money market or other account that pays a higher rate. Your parents can place any additional money in a certificate of deposit (CD) or other similar investment vehicle, which pays even higher interest in return for a promise to leave the money invested for three, six, nine, or twelve months, or longer. Your parents will want to balance the extra interest earned against possibly higher taxes on the earnings, as well as against the time commitment required. If your parents desperately need the money from a CD, they can obtain it by paying a penalty that can conceivably cancel out most of the interest earned to date. If you and your parents have drawn up a monthly budget, however, they will rarely be caught short.

Owning Stocks

Stocks can generate income two ways: by increasing in value and by paying dividends. Most stocks pay fairly low dividends. However, if your parents have enough money invested in stocks, their dividends can pay for a significant portion of their lifestyle. With low dividend stocks, your parents can sell some shares and use the money for living expenses.

If your parents plan to sell shares, they may want to sell some every month. This approach leaves them vulnerable to price fluctuations, and also increases the total commission cost for a given number of shares, particularly if they sell fewer than one hundred shares at a time. Depending on the impact of capital gains taxation, they may find it most efficient to sell shares infrequently — say, once a year — and invest the proceeds in a savings or money market account, or some CDs, until they want it. With this approach, they can sell whenever they feel the shares are at high prices. However, if your parents misjudge the market and sell before a major price increase, they could leave behind thousands of dollars.

Owning Bonds

For safety's sake elderly investors should own only the safest bonds (rated "A" or better by reliable rating services). Income from bonds can be either *taxable* or *non-taxable*. For income to be federally non-taxable, it must derive from some type of municipal, government, government-agency, or special-purpose public works bond. Income from these bonds may still be subject to state tax. Your parents can avoid state, as well as federal, income taxes by owning bonds their home state recognizes as tax-exempt.

Although bonds pay a very stable income, their current sales price, or market value, will change as interest rates move up and down. If your parents hold their bonds until maturity when bonds pay their full face value, price fluctuations should be of no concern, and there should be little or no danger of losing any money. Because income from bonds is normally fixed, however, inflation can severely erode its purchasing power over the course of time.

If your parents plan to sell a bond before it matures, price fluctuations can be of major concern. Certain bonds can be *called*, or redeemed before maturity by the issuer in what amounts to a forced sale. If a bond is called, your parents may be unable to replace it with an equally safe investment paying a comparable income.

Owning Mutual Funds

If your parents don't want to select individual stocks or bonds, they can own shares in a mutual fund. The fund generates income for its investors by owning stocks or bonds that pay income and/or increase in value. Most mutual fund income is taxable. But if the mutual fund owns tax-free or "double (federal and state) tax-free" bonds, the federal and state governments treat investors' income as though it came directly from these bonds.

Funds that invest in overseas stocks, bonds, or currencies sometimes pay higher rates of return than funds which invest only in U.S. assets. However, these funds will gain or lose in value whenever the *exchange rate* of the dollar changes. Thus, an exciting fifteen percent increase in an international mutual fund may be offset by a twenty or thirty percent decline in the value of U.S. dollars, leaving your parents with a net loss on their mutual fund investment. Obviously, international investing entails an extra risk which your parents may not want to accept.

Depleting Capital

Some aging parents feel very reluctant to meet monthly living expenses by dipping into the principal amount of their nest egg. They prefer the traditional retirement plan of living on their current income. Some talk about wanting to leave money to their children, while others are (realistically) worried about outlasting their financial resources and having to severely curtail their spending at some point in the future.

Living only on income is one way, but not the only way your parents can manage their finances. Since they won't live forever, your parents may be able to live more comfortably for many years by depleting a small portion of their capital at regular intervals.

From a practical point of view, the distinction between "living on capital" and "living on current income" has become blurred in modern times, anyway. The under-lying interest rate — three to four percent for safe invest-ments — has remained virtually unchanged for hundreds of years. However, inflation is now so well-anticipated that interest rates are set high enough to compensate for it. Your parents can save and reinvest this extra interest, rather than spend it.

Here's an example: Assume your parents receive ten percent on a $1,000 one-year certificate of deposit. Of that ten percent, three to four percent constitutes simple in-terest on the investment. The remaining six to seven percent "extra" interest is intended to make up for pur-chasing power lost due to inflation that takes place while their money is invested. If inflation is six or seven percent, at the end of a year your parents' $1,000 will buy only $930 to $940 worth of goods. They will have to use the $60 to $70 in "extra" interest to restore the full purchasing or investing power of their original $1,000. If they treat this extra money as ordinary interest income, however, and simply spend it, they're actually "living on capital." To live only on income in today's economy, your parents must save and re-invest all interest income in excess of three to four percent per year.

Supplemental Earnings

If your parents don't have enough net worth to sup-port the lifestyle they want through interest income, and if they are physically and mentally able, they may want to supplement their income with a job or small business. Millions of "retired" people don't actually stop working. They change careers. Your parents may be able to provide a service — such as gardening or typing — or may be able to work as "consultants" in a business or industry they know. If they can't actually manufacture, import or export a product, they may earn commissions selling products or services they believe in. However, be careful about encouraging them to take on a job. If their capacities are too diminished, your parents may not be able to handle the responsibilities or the pressure, and may suffer embarrassment and loss of self-esteem when a boss expresses disappointment in their work.

Living Expenses

Forecasting your parents' approximate living expenses while they remain healthy and self-sufficient is fairly easy. If they're already retired, they can make estimates based on past expenses. If they haven't yet retired, they'll want to make adjustments for anticipated changes in their lifestyle.

Retired people generally spend less on clothes, restaurant lunches and commuting. They may cut down on life insurance, move to a smaller, less expensive home, and give up a second car, with its heavy insurance payments and maintenance costs. However, they may spend more for hobbies, entertainment and vacation travel.

If your parents lose physical or mental capacities, their medical expenses can significantly increase. They may require more medicines and medical services, more support services for transportation and meals, and perhaps paid caregivers to make daily life more comfortable.

Start building your parents' monthly budget with costs for groceries and food (including meals out), clothing, laundry and dry cleaning, home maintenance, health and other needed insurance, and taxes on any income and any real estate they own. If they have a car, budget for fuel, insurance, and repairs. Don't forget telephone, water, electricity and gas. Most parents spend something on travel and entertainment, too. Health insurance premiums — for Medicare and possibly a supplemental "medigap" policy — can make a hefty dent in a retirement budget.

It's critical to consider inflation in budgeting for the future. Rent that's $500 per month this year can easily increase by four or five percent per year, on average. Similarly, the cost of everything from movie tickets to food and clothes generally goes up as time goes by. This means if $1,000 per month gives your parents an adequate income this year, in ten or fifteen years they may require $2,000 per month to buy the exact same lifestyle. If they can't take steps to increase their income from year to year, they may have to live less well or eat into their capital faster than they might like.

Your parents will probably make unrealistically low budget estimates. Don't let them. In most families, it costs parents far more to live than they expect. In the Browning family, for example, when George and Jeanette first retired they became afraid of overspending, and worked out a budget that would not eat into their nest egg. After ten years, however, they began feeling much more of a financial pinch than usual. With the help of their son, Arnold, an accountant, they discovered their expenses had nearly doubled since retirement, but their income had increased only fifty percent. They were able to ease the pressure somewhat by cutting back on some vacation travel plans and dining out less often, and by investing in some higher-paying bonds and mutual funds. But the Brownings were classic victims of the inflation squeeze that threatens everyone living on a fixed income.

Budgeting for "No Income" Periods

One of the challenges of assembling a budget for parents on a fixed income is that many bonds and similar investments don't pay on a monthly basis. Most bonds pay income only twice a year. Many CDs pay no income at all until they mature in three, six, nine, twelve months, or longer. In the intervening months, living expenses continue, so your parents must rely on long-term planning to cover their expenses.

The simplest way is to keep money in "tiers" of "timed" accounts. For example, son-in-law Bill keeps only a minimum of Mildred and Addison Williams' money for living expenses in a readily available checking account — no more than enough for the next month or two — because the account pays a fairly low interest rate. He uses other accounts, like CDs and similar higher-paying investments — which impose heavy penalties for withdrawals before specified dates — to hold other money earmarked for expenses in months to come. Bill schedules the permissible withdrawal dates carefully, so every month or two money flows into the Williams' regular checking account. When Mildred and Addison receive the next round of bond payments and other investment income, every six months or so, Bill sets up the same kind of "tiered" and "timed" accounts to cover their bills for the next "no income" period.

Even if your parents hold no bonds, they can set up a similar structure with their nest egg cash. For example, after setting aside enough to pay expenses for three months, it's easy for your parents to put twenty-five percent of their investment money into each of the following: a three-month CD, a six-month CD, a nine-month CD and a one-year CD. From then on, every three months at least twenty-five percent of their nest egg cash becomes available. In an emergency, they could use it to meet expenses. Most times, however, they can place as much as they will need for the next three months in their savings or checking account and lock the remainder away as profitably as possible in a one year CD or another safe vehicle.

Mad Money

Remember to encourage your parents to include some discretionary spending in their monthly budget. Money for incidentals — even just a couple of movies and a dinner out each week — will give your parents some latitude for extra enjoyment and help them avoid feeling financial pressure.

If they can afford it, your parents should also consider placing a more sizable sum — anywhere from one to eight weeks of ordinary spending — into a special "mad money" account. Don't let them stuff it in the mattress — it won't earn any interest there and inflation will erode its value. But they should keep this money readily available rather than locking it into a certificate of deposit. Of course, they'll forego a small amount of interest by keeping the cash so readily available, but that's a small price to pay for the freedom, excitement and enjoyment of having money for special expenses outside of budgetary constraints.

For example, George and Jeanette Browning like to use their "mad money" to visit the grandchildren on a birthday or anniversary, or to take a short vacation after recuperating from a bout with illness. Estelle Granger, age 80, uses the money for a new outfit or dinner in a special restaurant. Others give small portions of it as gifts to make their adult children's lives a little easier, or to mark events in children's or grandchildren's lives.

In the Kinney family, 72-year-old Cynthia scoffed at the idea of keeping "mad money" available for easy spending. But her daughter, Heather, absolutely insisted. Over the next few months, the widow said little about her small, but special account. However, one summer evening as the two women lounged on a balcony and sipped iced tea, Cynthia began discussing the possibility of taking a short ocean cruise. Eventually, she decided not to go. But all that summer and fall she broached many other ideas to her daughter. After more than a year, she still hadn't spent her mad money, but she'd had hours of pleasure considering the exciting things she could have done.

It doesn't really matter how your parents use their "mad money." Just having it available — even without using it — can make a difference in how they feel about themselves and their lifestyle.

Medical Expenses

One of the uncertainties of parenting your aging parents is that you never really know what tomorrow may bring. Accident, illness, or disability can strike at any time. Every change in Mom or Dad's physical or mental condition is usually going to cost money. There are many ways to anticipate and meet health care expenses for your parents. Proper planning — including adequate insurance — will make an important difference and can do much to reduce the burden.

Medical Insurance

Basic health insurance covers physicians' care and hospitalization. More comprehensive policies may also cover care provided at home, medical equipment, prescription drugs, eyeglasses, hearing aids, dental care, or long-term care in a skilled nursing facility (nursing home).

Medicare: As you may know, Medicare is health insurance from the federal government for Americans. It includes separate programs for hospital insurance ("Part

A," which covers hospitalization and some follow-up care) and for medical insurance ("Part B," which pays for doctors and other medical services and equipment). For detailed information on Medicare benefits, costs and eligibility requirements, contact your local Social Security office or the Health Care Financing Administration in Washington, D.C.

Medicare is one of the primary sources of insurance benefits for Americans over 65 and for some disabled Americans of any age. To be eligible, you generally must qualify for Social Security benefits. Medicare doesn't cover some of the initial costs of each illness, injury, or treatment program. In addition, there are continuing "co-payments" Medicare requires your parents to pay toward hospitalization and doctors' charges. The law requires a "co-payment" to help discourage people from seeking and accepting care they don't really need. Medicare pays for medicines only while your parent is hospitalized. There are also limits on the number of days of care for which Medicare will pay. Your parents must make their own provision to pay for services and treatment not covered by Medicare.

For most of your parents' regular medical care — check-ups and so forth, Medicare pays eighty percent of doctors' charges, but only of a standardized "allowable" amount established by the government for your geographic region. Your parents must pay the remaining twenty percent. Some doctors will charge more than the allowable amount, but many accept the government's payment guidelines — a process called "accepting Medicare assignment." It's prudent to verify *before* the first appointment that any physician your parents consult accepts Medicare assignment. Even though the physician charges only what Medicare publishes as its standard fees for specific services in your region, your parents will still be responsible for a co-payment.

One important fact of life is that, under Medicare, local insurance carriers — the "fiscal intermediaries" who process and pay claims — exercise a broad range of discretion in deciding exactly what services they will *and will not* pay for, unless explicitly laid out in the Medicare regulations. This makes for wide variations and inconsistencies between states as to the specific services for which Medicare patients are covered. Medicare can cover a procedure for a family member in another state, but deny your parents coverage for the same procedure.

If your parents are turned down for Medicare payment — which happens on routine claims not properly billed, on maintenance therapies for which restorative value must be substantiated, with medical equipment purchase or rental, and with new or non-routine medical services like investigational cancer therapies — this is not necessarily the end of the line. You can help them get their doctor's cooperation in submitting a more detailed bill, in requesting an explanation, in filing a formal grievance, and if necessary in appealing to the Health Care Financing Administration, which oversees the federal Medicare program. All of this involves exasperating delays, and, if successful, pays only the original benefit amount — without extra compensation for the delay, the expense, or the stress of making the appeal.

Medigap Insurance: Although Medicare is good primary coverage for most older people, many who can afford it opt for a special type of insurance coverage designed to cover the twenty percent co-payment requirement of Medicare. These "medigap" policies are entirely optional. You can find "medigap" policies designed for individuals and others for groups — such as employees or retirees of a certain company, or members of a particular union, organization, or association.

About twenty million elderly are reported to have some sort of medigap insurance (including many with more than one policy), but some may be getting less than they pay for. Because insurance companies have paid high commissions, sales people have been known to pressure people to purchase excess medigap insurance by exaggerating benefits and playing down the policy costs. Such abuses led to major concern by consumer protection organizations. In response to complaints that older people pay thousands of dollars in premiums for inadequate or duplicate medigap coverage, the federal government is demanding new regulations on medigap insurance. This includes restrictions against selling duplicate coverage or selling medigap policies to those who qualify for Medicaid, limits excessive sales commissions on policies, and standardizes coverage so you and your parents can more easily compare competing policies.

As with any insurance, there are complexities and difficult decisions regarding medigap coverage. Be aware that:

- Medigap coverage does not pay for everything Medicare excludes. Your parents can believe they are "fully insured" but still face hefty bills for services not covered by standard Medicare.

- Premium increases for the policy can be tied to advancing age.

- Guaranteed renewability (required by mid-1992) prevents the insurer from canceling the coverage just when your parents begin to need it.

- Your parents should choose carefully, because changing from one medigap policy to another can create difficulties, particularly with regard to pre-existing conditions.

- Most medigap insurance allows your parents to go to any doctor or other provider they wish. Some newer *preferred provider organizations* (PPOs) narrow a subscriber's range of choice for medical providers in order to secure discounts and lower overall costs. If your parents are willing to use these providers, this can be a good choice for them.

Supplemental Insurance: In addition to "medigap" policies, some families want coverage that can reimburse them for some of the costs Medicare never covers. Some private supplemental insurance policies can be expensive, however, and sales claims can exaggerate the benefits of such insurance and play down the policy costs. For example:

- The much-advertised "hospital indemnity" plans may be a poor bargain for your parents. The benefits sound large, but usually cover less than a tenth of the total cost of a hospital stay.

- Special cancer and heart disease policies may stack up poorly against full-coverage policies. Premium costs are often very high in comparison to the narrow range of conditions these policies cover.

- Your parents may have several separate policies that overlap. With this duplicate coverage, your parents might be paying several times for benefits they can receive only once, and in general may have more insurance than they need.

Before you or your parents buy any medigap or supplemental health insurance, compare several competitive policies on the basis of their waiting periods, exclusion of any existing health problems, allowable choices of physicians and hospitals, and duplication of coverage already in force. It's usually better to buy one comprehensive policy than many small ones, because this secures the most coverage and potential benefits for every premium dollar, and eliminates duplication of claims and other paperwork.

HMOs: If your parents do not have a personal physician, or don't feel it's important to select their own medical providers, they can obtain health care coverage in some regions of the U.S. from health maintenance organizations (HMOs). About 1.2 million Medicare recipients have relied on more than 200 different HMOs for their medical care during the last several years. Once your parents sign up with an HMO, Medicare pays that organization a fixed monthly fee. In return, the HMO provides your parents with medical care through one of its contracting physicians or medical groups.

Most HMOs offer at least two plans. The *basic* plan simply provides the care normally covered by Medicare. The *high option* plan offers an enhanced array of services, such as dental care, prescriptions and hearing aids, but costs your parents more per month.

To provide this care, the HMO hires or contracts with all the physicians, nurses, technicians and medical facilities its members are likely to need. If your parents want to go to a different doctor, or if they don't like the hospital to which the HMO directs them, they must pay their own way. The HMO will not provide reimbursement unless it is a true emergency and a regular HMO provider is not available.

Because the often excellent care of an HMO can be less expensive than conventional care backed by medical insurance, some families prefer this approach. There can also be much less paperwork because claim forms are eliminated as long as your parents stay within the HMO's provider network. On the other hand, HMO services are often less accessible, with fewer options.

Social HMOs are an experimental form of HMOs for seniors that provide a strong emphasis on individual case management, home assessments, home-based (rather than institutional) care, and several months of paid custodial care without requiring prior hospitalization. Monthly charges for membership in a Social HMO can be the same as for ordinary HMOs, or can run an extra $25 per month, or more. The idea is to increase efficiency by having the Social HMO substitute less expensive forms of care for traditional hospitalization or nursing home placement. At present, the first four Social HMOs are "demonstration projects" established by the U.S. Congress in 1984 and likely to be maintained at least through 1995. Additional Social HMOs may also be developed.

Before signing up with any HMO, it's important to understand:

- HMO doctors will tightly monitor and restrict your parents' access to health care within the system. Your parents won't be able to schedule an appointment directly with a specialist, such as an ophthalmologist for an eye complaint, for example. Your parents select a "primary care" physician or medical group that must specifically authorize the provision of every service.

- The HMO is a closed system. Your parents will have to accept treatment from physicians employed by (or contracted to serve) the HMO. The HMO may send your mother to its own heart specialist, for example, instead of a pre-eminent doctor at a large teaching hospital. Some HMOs have arrangements with top specialists, but severely restrict access to them.

- The HMO may refuse to reimburse for medical care provided outside of its service area, except in bona fide emergencies. Thus when your parents travel out of state, they may unknowingly leave behind much of their health insurance. If your parents make frequent or extended trips away from home, HMO plans are probably not a good choice for them.

- Your parents may have to endure delays for services, except in major emergencies. Remember, the U.S. General Accounting Office recently reported that "the incentives of a capitation payment system [as used in HMOs] may encourage the inappropriate reduction of necessary services." If members use too many services, the HMO loses money. For example, the primary care physician may not authorize an expensive Magnetic Resonance Imaging scan to spot the cause of Dad's back pain, although you feel it is warranted. Your parents may have to learn to "work the system" — who and when to call, and what to say — to get the care they want, and you may have to become a forceful advocate for them. Even when the primary care physician authorizes examinations or treatment by specialists, or expensive tests or procedures, many HMO services require "utilization review" — approval by a committee of doctors who meet regularly to consider such requests. Utilization review holds down costs, which is good. But your parent may have to wait days or weeks for the committee's decision.

- Medicare HMO plans must have established grievance procedures, often accessed by contacting "member service representatives." These measures help maintain quality and access to care. Don't be afraid to file grievances when necessary.

To lessen their risk, some HMOs are switching toward a "health care prepayment plan" approach. This can allow your parents somewhat more flexibility of choice, but can increase their out-of-pocket expenditures for health care services and hospitalization. It also gives the HMO more freedom to prevent individuals from joining after they develop chronic (and expensive) medical problems, such as end-stage renal disease.

Before your parents sign up with an HMO, try to talk with people already enrolled in the plan. Get their thoughts and personal experiences. You can also call the Department of Insurance (or the equivalent agency) where your parents live to ask about the financial stability of the HMO your parents are considering, and the number and kind of grievances filed against it.

Medicaid: This is a federally-sponsored and state-administered health insurance program for low income Americans. If they qualify, your parents may be covered by both Medicare and Medicaid. This eliminates co-payments and the need for private medigap coverage. Medicaid does cover the cost of long-term care. For information on Medicaid eligibility, benefits, and other details, your parents should contact their state's Medicaid office.

Long-Term Care

Although immediate care for your parent after an accident or illness can cost a lot of money, a much more potent threat to your parent's financial well-being is the steady drain of long-term costs. With all the benefits of modern medicine, people are now living longer, surviving even the acute illnesses that would have been fatal years ago. People who might have mercifully died after a short period of suffering may now linger in nursing homes for many years. Although many older people enjoy extra years of satisfying activity and relationships, others survive while only barely aware of their surroundings. They require constant care and attention — and they pay very high medical bills. In 1990, Americans spent over $40 billion on long-term care, and may spend three or four times as much per year in the next decade.

The cost of long-term care is not covered by Medicare and similar medical insurance, except for the first one hundred days after discharge from a hospital. Thus, your parent will almost certainly have to pay for long-term care using family funds or private "long-term care" insurance. Once these sources are exhausted, Medicaid may take over. However, Medicaid usually pays for long-term care only *in* a nursing home or other "skilled nursing facility." The heartbreaking reality is that this limitation may force your parent into a nursing home even when he or she could continue to lead a better, more independent and satisfying life at home, utilizing far less expensive help from attendants or other caregivers.

Many states require your parents to spend a large portion of their nest egg before they can become eligible for long-term care benefits from Medicaid. In too many families, one aging parent's chronic illness and lingering decline permanently impoverishes the other. In other families, the threat of poverty drives a caring couple to obtain a legal divorce in hopes of preserving some of their nest egg. The federal government recently began raising the "minimum net worth" guideline, and many states are changing their eligibility rules to prevent these financial tragedies, but the process is slow and bureaucratic.

Careful financial planning can help prevent long-term care from absorbing all your parents' assets. By knowing the eligibility limits that apply and disbursing funds well before long-term care becomes an immediate need, your family may be able to protect and retain considerably more assets.

Transferring assets to other family members is a common strategy. (For purposes of Medicaid eligibility, assets your parents transfer to joint ownership continue to count toward their net worth. Assets placed under formal trust arrangements generally do not count.) Done properly, asset transfers can reduce your parents' net worth enough to make them eligible for the government benefits they need. Many state agencies dispensing public benefits, however, now look for asset transfers made during the previous two or three years, and for eligibility purposes treat your parents' net worth as though these transfers never happened. Therefore, anyone who decides to pursue this strategy shouldn't delay.

Occasionally, a state government sues to recover its outlay for an elderly parent's long-term medical care, trying to seize assets it considers illegally transferred away. This process can be very upsetting and expensive for the family. However, by having all the proper documents signed and all the records accurate, you'll be able to defend such lawsuits more effectively.

To illustrate how unfair Medicaid eligibility rules can be, consider the experience of the Granger family. Dan Granger suffers from Alzheimer's Disease. Each month, Estelle Granger pays nearly three times the rent on her apartment to keep her husband in a nearby nursing home. Because their net worth is too high, the state does not help with this heavy expense. Under the rules, however, Estelle is legitimately entitled to deplete their net worth and make them eligible for state aid by taking an ocean cruise, spending lavishly on clothes and entertainment, and even gambling away some assets. Yet gifts to the Granger's adult children, Phil and Zack, or to their grandchildren — including money intended for college expenses or other important purposes — are not allowed under the eligibility rules.

A more frightening example concerns the Tidwells. At age 76, Bart had a major stroke that forced him into a nursing home before many of the modern protections against financial disaster were in place. After Medicare coverage ran out, his wife, Mary, spent all their savings to pay for his care. Before they qualified for Medicaid, she sold their house (a step that is avoidable under modern regulations), their car and their furniture. Now she rents a small apartment and lives from one Social Security check to the next, with no financial security and no hope of obtaining any. If Bart recovers from his stroke, he'll go home to an inadequate apartment, with no way to pay for care outside the nursing home. Their adult children help as much as possible, but the Tidwells have suffered a major financial tragedy precipitated by Bart's health crisis.

Long-Term Care Insurance: Some families try to anticipate the cost of long-term care with special purpose insurance. But no agency has established "standard" levels of benefits, so premiums for many long-term care insurance policies are extraordinarily expensive, compared with the true actuarial cost of the benefits they promise. Remember, these policies pay only for certain expenses resulting from certain health problems. Help your parents shop around for the most complete benefits package at the lowest premium. Unless your parents know exactly what to look for, they can pay much more and get considerably less than they might expect.

Before purchasing any private long-term care insurance, your parents should know exactly what limitations — if any — the policy places on the diagnoses it covers, and on whether they can receive long-term care at home, in any nursing home, or only in a licensed facility. They should also recognize and calculate the financial impact of the policy's time and dollar limits. For example, some policies specify maximum daily, monthly or annual benefits, yet nursing home costs increase every year. Most policies have a "lifetime maximum" on benefits to be paid. As mentioned earlier in this chapter, some policies cannot be easily renewed as your parents reach the ages when they are most likely to need coverage, while others have provisions for cancellation by the insurance carrier that make them virtually non-renewable.

"Pre-existing condition" restrictions and "riders" excluding certain conditions are difficult to understand with almost all health insurance. For long-term care policies, the exact wording of these restrictions can be crucially important. For example, some riders and restrictions severely reduce benefits for a few diagnoses, and may exclude Alzheimer's Disease or mental problems. Your parents should also consider such factors as:

- The waiting period (generally quite long) before the long-term care policy begins to pay benefits.
- The maximum benefit for one stay as well as the lifetime maximum.
- The policy's coverage for stays in intermediate and custodial care facilities. Look for specific coverage for home-based care.
- The requirements (if any) for hospitalization prior to placement in a long-term care facility.
- Whether or not the premium is waived while benefits are being paid.
- The potential for premium increases while your parents will want the policy.

- The limitations (if any) on renewability of the policy. "Guaranteed renewability" is best.
- The financial stability of the insurance company offering the policy.

Other Medical Expenses

In addition to the costs of outpatient care, hospitalization and long-term care, your parents may also have to meet other medical expenses. These could include one-time costs for medical assessments or evaluations, as well as special medical equipment, adaptive devices and unusual or "investigational" treatments.

Insurance may not cover these expenses. When it does, your parents may still remain responsible for some portion of the total cost.

Establish a Contingency Fund

Despite the best planning and the best luck in avoiding heavy medical expenses, a time may come when a large medical bill lands in your parents' mailbox. This is the reason it's important you help your parents provide a contingency fund to meet sudden, heavy expenses.

A contingency fund need not be cash or money in a special account. You or your parents can simply earmark a certain amount of readily available money to meet emergency expenses. Some families prefer to keep their assets in high-yielding money market or other readily accessible accounts. Others prefer to use short-term CDs or bonds where money is less accessible, and to maintain a sufficient line of credit with a bank, a credit union, or even a charge card. In the event of an emergency, they simply borrow to meet expenses, then repay the loan with cash from their locked-up assets as soon as a withdrawal opportunity rolls around.

Tax Issues

Whether your parents are millionaires or barely scrape by every month, tax issues deserve some consideration. There are two distinct aspects to investigate and plan for: taxes on current income, and taxes on each of your parent's estates.

Taxes on Current Income

Taxes on your parents' current income are usually straightforward. Adult children generally know basic tax considerations because they pay their own taxes every year. For the most part, your parents will pay federal and state tax on all their earned and unearned income, except any income from tax-exempt holdings such as municipal bonds.

However, your parents may be entitled to some special deductions written into the tax law. When Fred Hinckley and his wife sold their home and didn't buy another, for example, because they were over age 55 they qualified for a special one-time right to deduct from income as much as $125,000 of their profit on the sale.

Your parents can also deduct from taxable income many of their medical and dental expenses, and a portion of their health insurance premiums. Be sure they keep receipts for hospital expenses, prescription drugs, nursing help prescribed by a doctor, medical aids like hearing aids and their batteries, contact lenses and eyeglasses, transportation costs to and from any place they obtain medical care, and other such items. The federal tax law details exactly how much of their income they must spend on these items before any of these expenditures become deductible. Consult a tax professional for the latest regulations.

Sometimes it makes sense for you or another family member to claim your parents as "dependents" for tax purposes. This works particularly well if you are paying a higher rate of taxes than your parents, or when your parents have more deductions than they can use in a particular year. But be careful — the government generally demands you pay more than half their living expenses during the year, and sets forth other strict regulations about who can claim whom as a dependent, and when.

You can figure your parents' basic tax rate by estimating their taxable income and subtracting their deductible expenses — mortgage interest, medical expenses over a minimum amount, business expenses and so forth — for a full year. Check a tax table for their approximate tax rate. Make the same calculation for yourself and then compare tax rates to see if there's a saving if you claim your parents as "dependents."

The same type of calculation can help your parents decide whether to seek tax-exempt investments. For *taxable* investments, people paying thirty percent in taxes keep only $70 out of every $100 they receive, while people paying fifteen percent in taxes keep $85 out of every $100. So for a given taxable investment, people in the higher tax bracket actually receive less "after tax income" than people in the lower tax bracket. Most tax exempt investments are geared to attract people paying the highest tax rates and make less financial sense for those paying taxes at lower rates, as most older people do. When you calculate your parents' "after tax" income from comparable taxed and non-taxed investments, you may find they keep more income from taxable investments than from equally safe tax-free ones.

Estate Taxes

In addition to taxing their current income, *the federal government* may tax your parent's estate when Mom or Dad passes on. (Separately, your *state* may tax any inheritance that people *receive* from your parent, but that is the recipient's concern rather than your parent's.)

In general, one parent can leave any amount to the surviving parent without incurring a tax, but the maximum estate a parent can leave free from federal taxes to others (aside from a spouse) is $600,000. If your parents' net worth exceeds this limit, the second parent to pass away will leave a combined estate that is relatively unprotected from estate taxes.

Imagine a situation where your aging mother and father are worth more than $600,000. When your father dies and passes his half of the estate to your mother, there's no estate tax. However, when your mother dies sometime later, the portion of the combined estate exceeding the $600,000 limit is heavily taxed. Many families with large estates prefer a more sophisticated tax strategy in which each parent wills his or her half of the joint estate directly to the children. This provides a total effective deduction of $1.2 million, greatly increasing the total amount of the estate the family retains.

Another good technique to reduce the size of estates is to give assets away before death. However, there are rules limiting how much your parents can give away to escape estate taxes. Under long-held standards, for example, your mother and father can each give up to $10,000 per year to as many different individuals as they wish. Thus, if their estate is worth $2 million, they can bring the total down to the effective $1.2 million limit described above by giving away $800,000. One plan for accomplishing this is to give $20,000 per year ($10,000 from Mom and $10,000 from Dad) to each of their four children for ten years in a row.

If your parent gives more than $10,000 per year per person, the government will later include the excess amounts in his or her estate for tax purposes. As a practical matter, therefore, your parents realize no tax savings by giving more than the legal limit.

Another approach is to use life insurance death benefits to "cover" some or all of the estimated estate taxes, and thus to allow more of the parent's estate to reach those mentioned in the will. A special type of policy providing "second to die" coverage pays nothing when the first parent passes away, but pays when the second parent dies, covering some or all of the estate taxes. While premiums for this type of "estate tax" life insurance are very expensive, the special tax treatment many life insurance policies receive can bring the premium costs artificially low.

Estate tax advantages are also available through trusts, and the law makes special provisions for widows and widowers in the year the spouse passes on, and for the profits realized from selling a home.

Because the estate and inheritance tax picture is tricky and complex, and changes regularly as new laws and court rulings emerge, it's important to consult a tax expert. The right advisor can formulate a very effective tax-saving plan while making certain the family complies with all the applicable laws and regulations. Good tax planning in advance will ensure the government gets only its fair share of your parents' assets — and not a penny more.

Meeting a Shortfall

In many families, parents enter retirement with enough money to support themselves in reasonable comfort. However, as inflation steadily eats away at assets and income, they eventually find themselves facing occasional or chronic financial shortfalls. Your parents' quarterly or semi-annual income checks may arrive too late to pay some of their current bills. Or a solid source of income, such as stock dividends or repayments of a note they hold, may begin to dry up. Your parents' daily living expenses may also begin to exceed their regular income.

One of the big dangers for people on fixed incomes is that expenses can suddenly skyrocket way above their anticipated budget. Evelyn Morrison's sudden illness required intensive care in a hospital ward and then round-the-clock nursing. Dan Granger's death will require Estelle to pay for everything from funeral expenses to lawyer's fees, in addition to living expenses while waiting for probate and other legal affairs of the estate to settle.

Although being short of money is troublesome regardless of the circumstances, it's important to determine whether your parents' financial shortfall is short-term or long-term. The time frame as well as the causes of their cash problems will greatly influence the steps you take to find the needed money from other sources.

Meeting a Shortfall With Cash Reserves

The easiest and most convenient way to meet a shortage is to withdraw the needed money from a savings or money market account. The danger, of course, is that withdrawing too much money will cut your parents' regular income. If your parents are relying on their nest egg to produce income, every dollar of "capital" they spend will cost them a little bit of annual income for the rest of their lives.

The best basis on which to withdraw money from cash reserves to pay current expenses is that you expect to replace it from income you *know* you will receive. For example, Mildred and Addison Williams hold a bond that pays fifty dollars every six months. So they can safely withdraw up to fifty dollars from their cash reserves during those six months because they are confident they can replace the money with their next interest payment.

Meeting a Shortfall By Selling Assets

If your parents don't have enough cash in a savings or money market account to meet a financial shortfall, they can still tap their "nest egg" by selling some of their other assets. They may sell their home, their car, some stocks or bonds, a coin collection. One factor to consider when your parents sell an asset is that they'll no longer gain from further price increases. Your parents will want to choose carefully among the assets they have and sell one of those least likely to appreciate. Of course, it's better if they can sell something they don't use or won't miss.

In certain situations, your parents may sell a car or a painting for more money than they need at the moment. Although they can invest the surplus, they may still face some tough choices, as did the Ginsberg family. Joe, a retired engineer, recently sold an antique volume of poetry worth over $10,000 to meet a $1,500 doctor bill. Although he still gains some benefit from investment interest on the excess $8,500, the book is gone forever.

Meeting a Shortfall With Family Contributions

Brothers, sisters, children and grandchildren will frequently pitch in to provide enough extra money to see parents through a financial shortfall. There may be a family scene involving high pressure offers and stubborn refusals. Sometimes, however, you can find a reasonable compromise. One approach is to sell an asset — or borrow against it — within the family. Of course, many people are reluctant to take financial help from their family. Because older people are often embarrassed by their shortfall, they may let their lifestyle fall apart before asking for help. When enough financial pressure builds up, though, they may accept financial help from their family.

Remember: Sound financial planning can sometimes provide advance warning that a shortfall is possible in the near future. If your parents accept the figures that prove they won't have enough cash to meet anticipated expenses, they may more easily accept family help before they get into financial hot water.

Meeting a Shortfall With "Senior's" Discounts

One of the clear advantages of aging in America is the tremendous diversity of cash savings older individuals can enjoy by taking a "senior's" discount. A broad range of products and services, from National Parks admissions to electric, gas and phone service can be had for free, or for special rates. Airlines, hotels, bookstores, movie theaters and other businesses offer significant savings, often very broadly and generously.

As a rule, businesses don't advertise their discounts for "seniors." You or your parents will have to ask about them. Contact your state, county, or local agencies on aging to find out more about some of the specific "seniors" discounts from which your parents might benefit. One of the most important generally turns out to be discounts on prescription medicines. If you are over 50, you can enjoy many of these discounts yourself.

Meeting a Shortfall With Credit

If your parents already have a credit history and one or more credit cards, they may be fully prepared to use credit to meet a financial shortfall. If not, they should consider applying for a small bank loan and a bank credit card immediately. This will begin a credit history and make it easier to borrow money when they need it.

Most bank credit cards charge at least eight to ten percentage points above the so-called "prime" interest rate for loans and unpaid purchases. While still expensive sources of loans, some banks offer credit cards at about six percentage points above "prime," others at just four points over. To find them, you and your parents should check financial publications and ask for referrals from financial professionals. Credit cards are provided nationally, so the bank can be located almost anywhere.

Although potentially expensive, credit cards are a convenient way to meet short-term "embarrassments." Your parents can easily meet expenses by writing a check against their credit card. Although this usually starts accumulating the eighteen to twenty percent interest rate expense, they'll pay only seventeen dollars if they borrow $1,000 for thirty days at twenty percent. However, if your parents borrow many thousands of dollars this way and don't repay the debt until many months or years later, they will incur a very large interest expense that can begin to deplete their assets and compromise their quality of life.

It's smarter and far cheaper to use the credit cards only for purchases. Don't let your parents borrow cash and pay for an expensive prescription, a new piece of medical equipment, or a major appliance. Encourage them simply to charge the purchase directly to a credit card. Your parents can charge their clothes, their gasoline and many other everyday expenses. Because these are "purchases" rather than "loans," most cards allow a twenty-five to thirty-day grace period without interest. If your parents pay their credit card bill in full when it comes due, they'll effectively get an interest-free loan every month. The only expense will be the bank card's annual fee, for some cards as little as twelve dollars per year.

Meeting a Shortfall With Long-Term Loans

If your parents need to borrow larger amounts for longer periods, there are several cost-effective avenues they can follow.

Ordinary loans from banks may provide a good source of temporary funds. Most times, the lending officer will want to secure the loan with some tangible asset — normally stocks, bonds, or cash deposited in the bank. This kind of collateral can work well as the basis for a loan because your parents won't lose the income from the asset while they use it as security. In effect, it serves double-duty.

A more elaborate approach is for your parents to use the equity in their home. Millions of older Americans own their homes free and clear. Millions more have fairly low mortgages nearly paid off. If your parents have lived in their house for a while, chances are they have built up many tens of thousands of dollars in equity, or more. Rather than leave this money idle while they scrounge for cash from other sources, home equity loans or revolving credit lines allow your parents the comfort of living on their own money — money they have been accumulating for many years in the form of home equity. Your parents can borrow against this home equity in one of three ways: by increasing their existing "first" mortgage or trust deed, by getting a new "first" mortgage or trust deed, or by getting a new "second" mortgage or trust deed.

With any of these *loans*, they receive the full amount in cash, whether or not they intend to spend it right away. A variation on the same idea is the revolving home equity *credit line*, through which your parents borrow only as they need to and pay interest only on what they actually owe.

Newer forms of mortgage and trust deed loans are providing other ways to convert home equity into cash. Various types of "reverse equity" home loans, for example, require no repayment until your parents die or sell their home. These types of loans make a cash payment to your parents every month, and post the amount advanced, plus monthly interest, as a loan against their home equity. Eventually, the advances and interest due are repaid from the sale or refinancing of the home.

Because a "reverse equity" loan depletes your parents' home equity, it's important your parents are cautious in using one to pay for retirement and other expenses. The danger, of course, is that your parents may prematurely use up all their value in the house. At one time in this country, homes were virtually guaranteed to increase in value. Families expected price appreciation of five, ten, or fifteen percent per year. In recent times, however, many homes have begun to decline in value, or at least to hold steady rather than increase. If your parents borrow against equity faster than it increases, they are on a collision course with debt.

Life insurance is another possible source of borrowing. Many people have *whole* life, *variable* life, or *universal* life policies with premiums higher than the raw cost of *term* life insurance. The excess premium accumulates, earns interest, and commonly avoids taxes until withdrawn. This amount is called the policy's "cash value."

Most insurance polices with cash value have some provision for obtaining the money, either by surrendering the policy and receiving the cash value, or by "borrowing" the cash value — it really belongs to the policy-holder, anyway — and paying a relatively low rate of interest on the loan. Be cautious. If your parents surrender their policy while they still need life insurance, they may find the policy impossible to replace at a competitive cost. If they borrow against their policy, the loan amount directly reduces the face amount of the death benefit, and the borrowed money no longer earns interest within the policy. In most cases, life insurance can be an effective way to meet a shortfall, but the hidden costs of borrowing can be more than your parents might think.

Life Insurance

Almost everyone has considered life insurance at one time or another, and millions of people have purchased it. An army of sales people stands ready to sell a wide variety of life insurance policies.

Fundamentally, life insurance is a way to provide financial compensation for the death of the person insured. For this reason, the "death benefit" of a policy should reflect how much income a person's surviving family will need after his or her death. If they will have little or no other income, life insurance can create an "instant estate." If the family has enough income from other sources, there may be no reason to purchase any life insurance at all.

For families hard-pressed for funds, however, a slightly more expensive type of life insurance available in most states can provide early delivery of death benefits, rather than the more economical withdrawal of, or borrowing against, cash value. This "living benefits" policy allows Mom or Dad to withdraw a portion of the purchased death benefit — while still alive. To qualify for these withdrawals, however, your parent generally must be terminally ill or confined to a nursing home. At the death of the insured any remainder in the policy is paid normally.

For most families, the child-rearing years carry the heaviest expenses, and thus the largest requirements for life insurance. For example, if a young mother and her two children would need $50,000 per year to live should her husband die, and the family has enough savings to generate $15,000 per year, it might be prudent to insure his life for $350,000 — at ten percent interest enough to generate the missing $35,000 in annual income without depleting the principal. If five percent interest were a more likely yield, $700,000 would provide the needed income.

However, many retired people already have enough money — or nearly enough — to support themselves for the rest of their lives. If your parents are in good shape financially, they may need little life insurance. Regardless of need, though, some people like to maintain a small life insurance policy to cover the costs of a terminal illness, funeral expenses and other final expenditures.

Tax Advantages of Life Insurance

Tax advantages are entirely separate from the death benefit of life insurance. Historically, the federal government has treated excess premiums you pay to life insurance companies as tax-advantaged savings. For this reason, many people buy annuities, cash value life insurance and other investment products based on a life-insurance policy. Provided these tax laws continue unchanged, life insurance may be a good place for your parents to place some of their savings.

If your parents already have assets in life insurance products, they should compare the relative advantages of leaving it there against retrieving it and investing it elsewhere. In some situations, "cash value" life insurance is a good investment. In others, it cannot compete with other, equally safe investment opportunities.

For example, traditional *whole* life policies pay pitifully small interest rates on the accumulated excess premiums. Newer *variable* life and *universal* life policies pay higher rates of interest, but still lower than some other investments. In addition, both *variable* and *universal* life policies include management charges your parents may initially overlook. If you look deeper into these policies, you'll discover they actually function like mutual funds. If your parents don't want to use life insurance policies as investment vehicles, they can get virtually the same benefits by choosing from among several thousand such mutual funds now operating without the strict contribution and withdrawal limitations imposed on cash value life insurance. If tax savings are particularly valuable to your parents, they can choose one of the tax-free mutual funds, many of which outperform cash value life insurance policies.

Obviously, life insurance is complex and tricky. Your parents should make no hasty decisions on where and how to invest, or whether to restructure their current investments. Help them look at the implications of the various opportunities before they decide what to do.

Chapter 4

MEDICAL CARE

All of us are continually and irreversibly aging. Unfortunately, one of the consequences of aging is often chronic illness and the failure of organ systems within the body. According to a survey by the U.S. Congress, nearly eighty percent of Americans over the age of 65 have some kind of chronic health problem ranging from stiff joints and slight hearing loss to major heart or lung disease, near total mental deterioration and loss of personality.

The basic principles of geriatric care advocate restoring as much function as possible and allowing extra time for healing. A vital concern is to avoid treatments, tests, or hospitalizations that can make your parent's overall condition worse. Most important, good geriatric care recognizes that medical care must mesh with social, family, financial and psychological factors.

This book is no medical textbook; we don't describe everything in detail. But we do provide information to help you understand the illnesses your parents may suffer, and to help them obtain good care.

Physical Signs of Aging

Although everyone ages at an individual pace, there are definite physical changes you can expect to see in your parents. The degree of change varies from one person to the next, as do the emotional and psychological effects of these changes.

With age comes normal changes in the ability of the body to cope with demands made on it, to endure stress and to perceive the world. These physical changes can have profound effects on how well your parent copes with everyday chores from shopping and driving to making decisions and exercising ordinary judgment and common sense.

It works the other way, too. Emotional trauma, stress, disorientation, or loneliness can accelerate the physical signs of aging. For some parents, deterioration advances rapidly once it begins. They suffer doubly: first from their physical problems, and again from making the adjustments needed to cope with these problems — in particular, moving away from a well-established home and neighborhood. Although your intentions may be the best, putting Mom or Dad through major life changes sometimes seems to "upset the apple cart" and hasten the fall.

Here are some of the physical and mental conditions that may change with aging:

Vision: Most of our parents can see well enough to handle common household chores and the requirements of daily living. They can go to movies, read their mail and observe street signs when they drive. With aging, the normal eyeball actually changes shape. Your parents may begin to need reading glasses, and have some trouble focusing sharply on objects within two or three feet. Curiously, extremely nearsighted people may see better — and need a smaller correction in their lenses — as changes in the shape of the eyeball improve their ability to focus on distant objects.

The pupil may grow smaller and less flexible with age, letting in less light and impairing vision in dim lighting conditions. Eyes may also become more sensitive to bright lights and need more time to adjust to changing lighting conditions. Vision may deteriorate generally due to degeneration of the cornea. There may be changes in your parents' ability to see colors. Blues and greens may become less distinguishable, while perception of other colors remains unchanged. Many older people also experience "dry eye," an irritation due to decreased production of lubricating tears.

In a considerable number of people, aging brings cataracts (a clouding of the lens) and chronic glaucoma (increased pressure within the eye). Easily treated if discovered early enough, untreated cataracts and glaucoma can cause blindness.

Hearing: The ability to hear high-frequency sounds begins to slip away during the teenage years. By the time your parent reaches 60, 70, or 80, he or she may be entirely unable to hear a significant portion of the sound spectrum. Fifty percent hearing loss is quite common in older adults.

A related symptom is the "cocktail party problem," where your parents can't easily hear what is said to them because of other conversations or noises in the background. They may also begin to miss words and phrases in relatively quiet settings. Sometimes you can reduce the problem by turning off the TV, radio, or other background noises. Other times, you must speak slower and more carefully than usual, in a clear, strong voice.

With modern technology, physicians who specialize in ear diseases can sometimes prevent or reverse hearing loss. Hearing aids are particularly useful devices that can be well hidden yet work effectively.

Other Senses: The senses of taste, smell and touch begin to fail as the body grows older. This happens because the cells that trigger these senses — the taste buds, the olfactory receptors and nerve endings in the skin — begin to deteriorate or disappear. In practical terms, your parents may complain about tasteless food no matter how much effort you invest in preparing meals; may not smell leaking gas; and may not feel a dangerously hot shower or cook pot. Their direct contact with the world is less intense.

Brain: Brain researchers have concluded that the aging process diminishes the number of active cells in the brain. There are billions of cells in a typical brain, and the loss of a few thousand, or a few million, need not impair its functioning. Nevertheless, your parent's brain and nervous system will probably begin to slow down as the years pass. Mom or Dad may become forgetful, especially about recent events. They may forget certain people, or words for common objects. They may repeat themselves, may not understand concepts as easily and quickly, and may have a harder time solving problems or functioning creatively. Since the brain controls muscles and receives stimulation from the nerves, perception and motor control also tend to diminish.

Heart and Lungs: Age makes the chest wall more rigid, reducing efficiency in the hearts and lungs. Blood — which becomes more anemic — will flow more slowly, less air will be exchanged in the lungs, and the net result will be lower amounts of oxygen reaching the cells. You'll see this manifested as general fatigue and less endurance. Your parents will grow a little weaker, less able to do work, and will require more rest. All this makes many older people prone to chronic disabilities and diseases:

arteriosclerosis, high blood pressure and strokes. Since older people tend to drink less liquid, secretions in their lungs may be thicker and more prone to infection. Because they are less active, they can be more susceptible to pneumonia and other illnesses. Many older people have heart attacks, congestive heart failure and other heart problems. For the elderly, heart attacks can initially appear very similar to other problems, such as indigestion or back pain.

Teeth: Humans develop only two sets of teeth. However, our "permanent" teeth often wear out while we still need to eat. The best medicine for teeth is good preventive care. Once their teeth are gone, your parents will have to wear dentures, or adjust their diets to softer foods with good nutritional value. Loss of teeth coupled with an inability or unwillingness to wear dentures sometimes contributes to malnutrition and general physical decline.

Digestive System: As the body slows down, your parents may have a harder time digesting their meals. Many medications, as well as foods they once enjoyed, will begin to cause stomach upset or other digestive problems that contribute to reduced appetite. In addition, feelings of loneliness, depression, or worry may create ulcers or other problems in your parent's digestive tract. As colon muscles weaken, constipation becomes a problem in about thirty percent of those over the age of 65.

Urinary System: Both men and women tend to have urinary problems as they get older. Kidney function and excretion of body wastes decline significantly. Decreased bladder capacity, more frequent spontaneous bladder contractions, decreased warning of a full bladder, urinary obstructions, weaker sphincter muscles and more frequent urinary infections all contribute to the increased incidence of incontinence. Men often suffer from prostate enlargement and related problems, women from bladder problems. They may inadvertently release some urine as they sleep, laugh, sneeze, or cough.

Skeleton and Muscles: Your parents may lose height as their vertebrae shorten and the disks between them thin out. Their posture may slump or stoop, their joints may stiffen and they may lose some fine motor coordination. They may also lose as much as half of their muscle mass, giving them a "withered" look and further contributing to general weakness. Diminished muscles and cartilage in the larynx contribute to the older person's characteristic high-pitched, tremulous voice. Because parts of the body become less elastic and flexible, your parents may complain of foot problems, as well as joint and back pains. Calcium loss can make your parents prone to bone — especially hip — fractures. Arthritis is also common.

Skin: The body's largest organ becomes thinner, drier, more transparent and less elastic with age. It may droop, sag, wrinkle, or form dark spots. The skin also suffers when other organ systems break down, and becomes more susceptible to skin cancer, ulceration and even gangrene. As the walls of the tiny blood vessels under the skin weaken, the slightest bump or blow may produce dark, unsightly bruises.

Endocrine System: Age changes the balance of hormones and other chemicals within the body. One problem is hypothyroidism, which can result in significant degrees of depression, lethargy, hoarseness, weight gain and dry skin. The pituitary gland can shrink and begin varying its rhythmic release of hormones. Men produce less testosterone, women less estrogen and progesterone. Diabetes is another frequent consequence of aging, often related to weight gain, frequent urination and thirst.

Emotions: Your aging parents may go through unusual emotional turmoil, including feelings of loneliness or apathy. As many as fifteen percent of elderly people suffer from depressive symptoms. Some parents will have these feelings because they have lost dear friends, or because illness or injury have cut them off from traveling and socializing. But for others, these emotions arise without much external stimulation. Either way, these feelings can interfere with sleep, appetite and activity levels. If they persist, these emotions can actually shorten lives.

There may be other changes as well. Organs lose weight and capacity; lean muscle is replaced with fat. Physical problems or side effects of medications may disrupt your parents' sexual drive and patterns of intimacy, but sexuality can and often does continue well into old age.

Treating Your Parents' Problems

It's always a good idea to help your parents overcome as many of the practical limitations on them, and pursue as many realistic opportunities as possible. Activity and social interaction will go a long way toward reducing the danger of isolation, loneliness and depression.

Health Care Professionals

You can't treat your parents alone. Your most important contribution is to help your parents find the appropriate resources and the right group of health care professionals — specialists who understand the needs of the elderly and their families. Geriatricians, gerontologists, many internists and family practitioners are specially trained and sensitized to recognize and deal with problems of the elderly that can hide behind the "obvious" symptoms.

Help your parents find doctors who essentially agree with their values, beliefs and preferences. Getting doctors who are on your family's side eliminates a lot of the wrangling, uncertainty and recriminations that can occur when parenting your aging parents. It also helps for you to establish a working relationship with your parents' doctors, so you can more easily step in when your parents need help.

Medications

A steady regimen of medication is one of the most common treatments for the elderly. People over 65 consume nearly a quarter of all medicinal drugs. Because of multiple conditions and chronic symptoms, they often take several preparations at once for long periods of time. In addition to over-the-counter drugs they self-prescribe, your parents may take medicines their doctors prescribe to treat illness, postpone expensive or painful diagnostic procedures, and even simply to quiet complaints. With so much medication passing so many lips, the potential for error and confusion is enormous.

Here are a few tips to keep in mind when helping your aging parents with their medications:

- Ask your parents' doctors to give clearly written instructions with every prescription. Your parents may not remember all the details of what medicine to take and when to take it, particularly when they are feeling ill. If the doctor balks, encourage your parents to find someone more concerned about their well-being.

- When filling a new prescription, your parents should give the pharmacist a list of all other medications they are taking, including over-the-counter (non-prescription) preparations. That way, the pharmacist can possibly anticipate and prevent any adverse interactions. Ask your parent's primary physician to perform the same safety check.

- Encourage your parents not to get their medications in "child proof" containers, which aging hands may have difficulty opening.

- Monitor their medication carefully, because many older people forget to take their dosages or take them twice. Studies show that almost sixty percent of elderly patients make medication errors.

- Provide a pill container with compartments for every day of the week. You, a nurse, or someone responsible can place Mom or Dad's necessary pills in the compartments. If they see the compartment is full, they know to swallow them. If the compartment is empty, they know they have taken their medication.

- Aches and pains can lead an older person to take an over-the-counter painkiller as well as an anti-inflammatory medication, which can cause gastro-intestinal bleeding. People suffering from constipation may take too many laxatives for good health. Monitor all the medicines and dosages your parents take.

- Be alert for drug reactions as well as ordinary illness. Consider medication reactions as the source of any new symptoms.

- Stopping a medication at the right time is just as critical to good health as starting it. Destroy old medication so your parents do not ingest it inadvertently.

The Medical Evaluation

Arranging for a thorough medical examination and evaluation is one of the first steps in assuming responsibility for helping your aging parents. It should assess their physical and mental status to provide a baseline from which to judge your parents' future fluctuations. It will also help you and your parents' doctors rule out — or rule in — specific reasons and conditions for behavior and emotional patterns, helping doctors to determine which conditions and problems are treatable and which are not.

In addition to a complete physical examination, a good medical evaluation will include a thorough functional assessment of your parent's abilities in several basic areas:

- How well does your parent see, hear, rise, stand, walk, talk, eat and sleep?
- Can your parent dress, and manage bladder and bowel functions without help?
- How well does your parent cope with everyday situations?

In many families, a parent will lose one or more of these abilities and be driven to depression, or other emotional turmoil, without knowing the root cause. Diagnosing the problem can often lead to an immediate and effective remedy — including anything from eyeglasses, hearing aids, or simple adaptive devices to medication and surgery. Doctors now believe that most disabilities of old age result from disease, and are preventable or manageable.

Major memory loss, intellectual decline, and confusion often show up as garbled or complete loss of speech, or inability to name objects. Such symptoms — while among the most distressing associated with aging — are not inevitable. More than eighty percent of aging Americans do *not* develop them. However, if your Mom or Dad does exhibit them, a good functional assessment can help differentiate whether the problems stem from physical causes or other factors. These problems generally appear in one of three distinct patterns which can help point to the cause: *new symptoms* in a previously healthy person, *suddenly worsened symptoms*, or *chronic symptoms* that change very little from month to month.

Safety is also a key issue. If your parents can't see well enough, they may take the wrong medication or the wrong amount. If they have trouble hearing, they may not know the phone or the doorbell is ringing, or may miss the sound of a smoke alarm, or a warning shout. If your parents regularly drive a car, a medical evaluation and functional assessment could pinpoint problems that compromise safety, or it could give them a clean enough bill of health to keep their automotive independence intact.

The comprehensive medical evaluation can be done by a good geriatrician or other elder-medicine specialist, or by a team of medical specialists working through a hospital-based geriatric assessment program. To find a physician or evaluation team, try calling a medical staff office or physician referral service at a teaching or university hospital. (Remember, hospitals refer patients only to their own staff physicians.) You can also ask your local medical association, your own personal physician, or a social worker at a large hospital in your area. Make sure the physician your parents select has *admitting privileges* at a hospital you respect.

You may want to discuss your parents with the physician a day or two before the examination and evaluation. First of all, make sure the doctor understands you want a complete evaluation, which will require more time than a typical office visit. Second, give the physician some clues regarding your parents' problem areas to help him or her focus on what may be the most important areas for evaluation.

Before your parents go to their appointment, sit down with them and make a list of all their symptoms, including the vague ones like general fatigue or weakness. Also list major illnesses, both long- and short-term, and all previous surgeries. Collect all the medical information you have and write down the names, addresses and phone numbers of previous doctors who may have formal medical records concerning your parents. Make a list of all your parents' prescription medicines including the names and dosages, as well as a list of vitamin or dietary supplements and non-prescription medicines, so the physician will have a complete picture.

As part of the evaluation, a good doctor will take a complete medical history to provide clues to hereditary conditions and risks. He or she will also consider what your parents eat, foods they can and cannot digest, how well they shop and cook for themselves, and their sleeping habits, as well as other details: do they run their own errands, clean their own home, pursue interests and hobbies, or work? All this presents clues to the trained eye that help pinpoint the exact level of functioning your parents retain.

Don't automatically assume you will sit in on this examination. Ask your Mom or Dad how they feel about it, and respect their answer. The physician or medical team may also have preferences for conducting the evaluation with or without you.

If you witness this examination, control your impulse to answer for your parent. It's important for the doctor or evaluation team to communicate directly. Each response provides clues to your parent's mental and physical status. You might even be surprised by some of what Mom or Dad says!

When the medical evaluation is over, don't expect instant answers from the physician. He or she may need weeks to receive all the lab results, review all the medical records and make a thorough evaluation. Expect to schedule a follow-up visit after the facts are in, at which time the doctor or an evaluation team member should be ready with a complete assessment of your parent's present condition, as well as a treatment plan.

Make sure both you and your parents — if they are able — understand every aspect of the diagnosis and assessment. Ask any questions that come to mind. If you're confused or dissatisfied with any part of the treatment plan, don't be afraid to raise questions or objections — particularly to surgeries and other invasive or expensive procedures (like bypass surgery or angiography — which involves inserting a tube in a vein or artery). Later, at home, you and your parents can consider and discuss the evaluation report.

One way to increase your satisfaction with the assessment or treatment plan is to get a similar evaluation from another physician without disclosing the first set of results. Your parents' insurance may pay to obtain a qualified second opinion.

When the examinations and assessments are done, you should have a complete picture of your parents' physical and mental condition. You'll know what diseases and disabilities they have, how they may progress through the next few years, and the medical treatments and other interventions your parents may need.

Armed with this information, you can begin working to address any special or acute problems needing immediate treatment. You'll also be able to work toward maintaining the highest level of functioning possible for your parents, and to prevent as much further decline as possible.

Health Maintenance for Your Aging Parents

Maintaining your parents (or helping them maintain themselves) in the best possible health should always be one of your primary goals. This entails more than attending to chronic problems, accidents and illnesses. It requires that you develop a baseline of medical examinations and evaluations, and then follow with regular check-ups. You'll also have to hone your powers of observation and evaluation.

Many problems of older patients are difficult to discern. Elderly parents will often attribute aches and pains to normal aging, and won't bother to report them. Yet doctors can frequently treat joint pain, hearing or vision loss, dizziness, falls and incontinence quite successfully. Older people can also forget or ignore their symptoms, or fail to notice even serious problems. They are often less sensitive to pain and may not complain about a heart attack or other acute condition. Furthermore, symptoms of some diseases, such as hypothyroidism, can be overlooked in older people.

Another serious diagnostic problem is that many older people with an underlying illness — even a mild one — outwardly exhibit a catastrophic decline. Because their health can be so precarious, they may begin falling frequently, become incontinent or disoriented. Doctors commonly focus on these obvious symptoms, which may be mere indications of an entirely different problem. Precarious health also makes the older patient highly susceptible to infection, trauma, and side effects of medication.

The common approach to health maintenance for aging parents has long been to select a primary care physician — a specialist in family medicine, internal medicine, or geriatric medicine — and to pay for regular and necessary visits and other care. Medicare eligibility and the purchase of supplemental medigap insurance traditionally helped protect against large medical bills and charges for surgery and hospitalization. However, health care costs regular rise faster than family incomes or inflation. In a recent year, for example, the costs for an average family rose eleven percent, more than twice the inflation rate. This means government insurance supplemented by a medigap policy may no longer be the best option for some families. In some areas of the U.S., HMOs (Health Maintenance Organizations) may offer "senior plans" that replace both government and private medigap insurance, and may offer extra benefits. [See Chapter 3 (Finances).]

Bear in mind that these choices are more than merely financial. They have significant impact on your parents' medical care: where and how they get it, who provides it, how timely they receive it, their relationship to those providing the care, and so forth. Don't wait for a crisis to spur you into action. Evaluate the options before your parents must make a choice. Learn all you can about the benefits and limitations of each plan, about the bureaucracies and the red tape.

Preventive Efforts

Good care for your parents involves more than patching them up after medical problems occur. You'll want them to take strong preventive measures against everything from pneumonia to sexually transmitted diseases.

Be sure your parents are getting good nutrition and following good health habits. When teeth go bad, hands shake, and other capacities begin to fail, it's often very easy to lower standards for eating and hygiene.

Encourage your parents to stay as involved as possible in productive activities providing social interaction and regular exercise. This helps preserve their level of functioning. Although they will probably lose some of their endurance, flexibility and coordination, they can retain much of their strength. As they grow older, your parents may want to change the nature of their exercise and activities, replacing aerobics or other strenuous action, for example, with swimming in a heated pool. But they should stay active. The general rule for aging parents is: "Use it or lose it!"

Caring for Illness in Your Parents

Both minor and major systems in your parents' bodies weaken with age and eventually begin to fail. People over 65 years of age generally require far more medical care than younger people. They suffer more acute problems (such as falls, broken bones and heart attacks) that require immediate care, and more chronic problems (such as arthritis and diabetes) that require ongoing medication, medical supervision and treatment.

Falls

According to the National Safety Council, injuries cause more deaths among the elderly than either pneumonia or diabetes. Five percent of deaths among the elderly — or about half of deaths due to injuries — result from a fall.

Women are generally more prone to falls than men. Those at special risk for injurious falls include about thirty percent of women over 65 and about fifty percent of women over 85, but only about ten percent of men over 65, and about thirty percent of men over 85.

Common causes of falls include the obvious: poor lighting, steep stairwells, obstacles on floors, loose rugs or wires, and faulty or slippery handrails. But there can be other, less obvious causes, including dizziness, cardiac and neurologic disease, functional disability, Parkinson's symptoms, or general poor health. There can also be sudden or chronic perceptual disorders, balance problems, or temporary circulation problems that cause an unexplained sudden fall called a "drop attack." The elderly in institutions are most prone to falls, even in such everyday situations as getting into and out of wheelchairs, beds, or simply walking.

A fall is bad enough. If it is onto fire, broken glass, or scalding liquids, it can cause great injury. If a person falls and cannot rise, there can be danger of pressure damage to the skin. Outdoors, there is risk of dehydration and, eventually, exposure. A fall can lead to other complications: bruising, chronic pain, broken bones, and long recovery and rehabilitation periods (which can lead to other health problems). As a result of past falls, some people develop strong fears about walking or climbing stairs, getting into or out of cars, and in extreme cases, simply standing alone. This fear can translate into reduced mobility, which can lead to further deterioration of general health.

Falls can be controlled and reduced by identifying and dealing with their causes. Make sure your parent's physician gets all the particulars about every fall and evaluates Mom or Dad immediately to see if anything can be done to prevent a recurrence. When falls happen frequently, a carefully planned rehabilitation program can help eliminate many problems and educate your parent to avoid or compensate for environmental dangers.

Incontinence

Several million Americans young and old, including perhaps as many as forty percent of those over 65, have lost some control over their bladder and bowel functions. If this happens to your parent, it can become a major family problem, putting a great deal of extra pressure on caregivers, as well as on your parent. Incontinence is often the final factor that forces the family to place your parent in a nursing home. When incontinence occurs, Mom or Dad can feel very distressed, and may refuse to discuss the problem or attempt to find a cure. To avoid any chance of embarrassment, your parent may limit social contacts and stay home as much as possible. Incontinence also brings risk of infection and skin ulceration. If the problem worsens, there may be no choice but to place Mom or Dad in some form of institutional housing.

Incontinence is not strictly a diagnosis, but a symptom of underlying disease or medical problems. It is frequently reversible, particularly when treated immediately. Some specialists estimate as many as ninety percent of incontinence victims can be cured or significantly helped. Surgery or medications can bring major improvement. Often a change in medication given for depression, insomnia, agitation, Parkinson's Disease, or other causes will eliminate the problem. Some aging Americans can learn to improve bowel and bladder control through behavioral training and biofeedback (in which electronic devices help them learn to use particular muscles more effectively). When appropriate, it's easy to purchase and use adult diapers, which greatly ease the distress of this problem.

Surgery

Medical problems of aging Americans frequently lead to surgery — sometimes too frequently. The vast majority of the more than nine million surgeries every year in the U.S. are performed on those over 65. Most work out well. But some operations are unnecessary. A Rand Corporation study, for example, found that of procedures performed by general surgeons to remove blood clots in neck arteries, only forty percent were necessary, including only twenty-eight percent of those performed by specialists. Only about seventeen percent of coronary (heart) and gastrointestinal (stomach or bowel) angiographies (tube insertions) were needed. Whether necessary or not, some operations lead to unhappy endings — no improvement, undesirable side effects, worsening of the condition, or even death.

For this reason, it's foolish for your parents to place themselves in a surgeon's hands without first fully understanding the problem, the surgeon's intended solution, the alternatives and the likely outcome from each possible course of action. Before you or your parents sign anything or agree to any invasive procedures, make sure the family understands:

- The diagnosis.
- The exact operation the surgeon plans to perform.
- The expected benefits of the operation, and the success rate for patients of similar health history, age and other variables.
- The risks of the surgery and the chances your parent will experience a complication.

- The expected course of recovery from the surgery.
- The total costs of the treatment, including: hospital, surgeon, anesthesiologist, radiologist, pathologist, other specialists, recovery and rehabilitation, and the applicability of your parents' insurance coverage. (Make sure your parents obtain all required authorizations, so they don't risk losing their reimbursement.)
- Alternative treatments, with their corresponding risks, outlooks and costs.
- The expected events if no surgery is performed.

Unless your parents are facing an emergency, it's probably wise to get another physician's opinion *before* agreeing to surgery. To find other physicians who can help you determine whether your parent should undergo surgery, ask their regular doctor for referrals. Also, call the local or state medical association and ask for the names of physicians who can provide a second opinion on your parent's present condition.

Make sure the doctor who determined your Mom or Dad needs surgery sends the medical records to the physician who will be offering the second opinion. This will save your parent the inconvenience and cost of duplicate tests. It will also speed up the process of getting the second opinion.

If the second doctor agrees surgery is warranted, you can go ahead with greater peace of mind. If he or she disagrees, however, and suggests another course of treatment, you and your parent may have to decide according to your own preferences and wishes. You're still better off, however, because you'll probably have more information about the problem and the possibilities for treatment than you did before. If you can afford it, you may want to obtain several subsequent opinions. In some complex cases, you may be able to find a specialist with wide experience in cases like your parent's, who is confident about undertaking the type of treatment about which your parent feels best. However, don't let any search for a doctor become primarily a way for Mom or Dad to avoid decisions or gain attention.

In recent years, Medicare and insurance companies have placed a growing emphasis on "outpatient" surgery — performed in a doctor's office, surgery center, or hospital without an overnight stay. For an elderly person, this requires the family to provide specialized care and support after discharge. (Your parent's physician may recommend hospitalization, if only to monitor your parent more carefully during recovery.) Unfortunately, as many as ten percent of doctors don't inform their elderly patients about the importance of follow-up care and the possibility of complications from outpatient surgeries. Some patients even go home alone. Before agreeing to outpatient surgery, make sure you know what you and other caregivers will have to do, what vital signs to monitor and what care and treatment to provide. Get a complete set of aftercare instructions *before* your parent agrees to the procedure, and make sure to line up caregivers with the resources and stamina to follow them.

Despite the risks and extra family effort required, the overwhelming majority of older persons prefer outpatient over inpatient medical care. In fact, outpatient surgery can be a good idea for an aging parent because overnight (and especially extended) stays in hospitals can contribute to confusion and disorientation. In addition to the stress of surgery and anesthesia on the body, hospitalization places severe emotional stress on your parent. In unfamiliar surroundings, with bland food, new medications, noise, and strangers coming in and out of the room all night, your parent may actually lose ground. In hospitals, there is also some risk of infection despite the most sterile techniques.

Any surgery involves the possibility of blood transfusions. In recent years, many people have become alarmed at the potential for transfusing diseases, particularly AIDS, along with the blood. This is a very remote possibility. Screening techniques have improved greatly in recent years, and experts consider at least this nation's blood supply to be extremely safe.

Of course, you'd prefer that your parent not receive a transfusion, but they are necessary sometimes to keep up strength, shorten recovery times and lessen any depression that might follow surgery. If your parent may need a transfusion, family members with the same blood type may want to donate blood and have it earmarked for Mom or Dad. Only after it becomes certain that your parent won't need the blood is it made available to other patients.

Many older people are on daily aspirin therapy, either a high dosage for arthritis or a low dosage to help prevent heart attacks and strokes. Aspirin thins the blood and hinders the process of clotting, both very undesirable factors during surgery. Talk about this with your parent's surgeon, who will probably recommend that Mom or Dad stop taking aspirin long before the operation.

Hospitalization

At certain times, illness, injury, or the need for surgery will force your parent into a hospital. Be careful about this. As many as 600,000 people each year are hospitalized unnecessarily, at tremendous financial cost and great risk of infection. Be as certain as you can that hospitalization is required before allowing Mom or Dad to be admitted.

Especially if your parent is slightly disoriented or fearful, before the day of admission it's important to go over where and when they are going, how long they are going to stay, what will happen to them in the hospital, and when you expect to visit. Bring some personal items, such as books, magazines and family pictures, even if the hospital objects to them wearing their own robes and sleepwear. While Mom or Dad is in the hospital, try to get all the people providing care to introduce themselves to your parent and explain what they are doing.

Closely monitor the care your parent receives. In hospitals with nursing shortages your parent's medication can arrive late. Staff can also treat your parent insensitively. If Mom or Dad is disoriented or fearful, she or he may be unable to speak up or may lose control emotionally. Function as a go-between, helping the staff work with your parent and steadily advocating your parent's needs and desires. Be sensitive because you're in a delicate position. If you're too demanding, you may make hospital staff angry or short-tempered with your parent and you. However, don't stand by and let inappropriate care go uncontested.

Differentiate between problems in nursing care and physician care. Discuss your problem directly with the doctor if he or she seems at fault. The doctor may help you present your other complaints to hospital staff. In many facilities, staff will listen to complaints from your parent's doctor more readily than from family. Instead of haranguing floor nurses or aides, speak to a supervisor or head nurse. If you're still dissatisfied, take your complaint to the nursing director or hospital administrator. Stay alert and save your biggest confrontations only for the most dangerous conditions, such as failure to respond to a medical crisis, or attempts to give your parent some incorrect medication.

Try to visit your parent as often as possible. Mealtimes may be best, because you can help your parent eat and verify what and how much they ingest. Unless their life is in danger, a few short visits are better for your parent than staying all day. Away from the hospital, you can also regain your composure and keep your own life — and your family's — from falling apart. As appropriate, discourage visits from anyone other than family members, and ask people to visit one or two at a time, for short periods. Flowers and get well cards will help to brighten the room, but hold off on candy. Your parent probably won't want it, and candy may entice visitors to stay too long.

Throughout your parent's hospitalization, maintain good communication with your parent's doctor. Time visits to his or her schedule at the hospital, or talk regularly by telephone. Ask questions. Get progress reports. And begin *discharge planning* early.

Discharge planning is the process of arranging for the most appropriate care for recovery after hospitalization. Talk to the hospital's social service or discharge planning staff about your parent's needs. With help from the staff, make arrangements as soon as possible for transportation and either a bed in a skilled nursing facility or home equipment and home health care, as appropriate. The hospital itself may offer some important services you can use. Today home health care agencies also make it possible to provide very sophisticated therapeutic regimens at home. Help Mom or Dad make the transition from the hospital as smoothly as possible by discussing all these arrangements with them well in advance.

Depending on your parent's condition, the hospital may send Mom or Dad home or to an intermediate care facility (which can be in or near the hospital or in a nursing home). Doctors usually prescribe intermediate care for a fixed number of days or weeks, and Medicare normally covers some or all of the cost. Your parent's course of post-hospital care may include some physical, respiratory, nutritional, speech or occupational therapies. Plan thoroughly and far in advance for your parent's release from intermediate care.

When your parent comes home to recover, inquire about any special requirements. For example, Dad may be confined to bed for a week, and may be forbidden to climb stairs for another month after that. You may have to adapt living spaces to your parent's rehabilitative needs. You can arrange for nursing care through a registry or a service based in the hospital. Home care agencies or visiting nurse associations will also help you care for your recovering parent. If the physician prescribes nursing care or special equipment, Medicare or private health insurance may cover it.

During all these unsettling experiences, Mom or Dad may be in pain, confused, angry, combative, or resistant to cooperating with necessary procedures. Try to understand these feelings. Don't argue. Soothe and reassure them as much as you can, but don't fall into the trap of doing unnecessary things for them. Sensitive outsiders, like hospital social workers who have knowledge and training unclouded by your level of emotional involvement, can often help you and your parent get oriented and handle these problems somewhat better.

Rehabilitation

Your parent's recovery from some illnesses, accidents, or surgeries may involve short-term or long-term rehabilitation. Even a simple surgery or minor illness can lead to significant deterioration. Specially trained therapists in a wide variety of specialties — such as physical, occupational, cardiac, respiratory and recreational — can work with your parent in the hospital, the intermediate care or skilled nursing facility, or at home. Their mission is to help Mom or Dad regain or attain a higher level of functioning.

Support these therapists' efforts and become involved in the program of care as much as your own busy schedule allows. Your parent may still be in pain or feel weak and unable to cooperate. Encourage Mom or Dad to work hard and do as much as they can, and to maintain a positive, optimistic attitude. Talk with the therapists about treatment plans and goals. Tell them about your parent's emotional state and compliance with treatment. The more your parent takes an active role in his or her own recovery, the quicker the rehabilitation and the better the overall outlook.

Medicare may pay for some or all of the needed rehabilitation services, particularly if your parent's physician prescribes and monitors the rehab program.

Hospice

One alternative for terminally ill parents is to place them in hospice, or arrange with a home health care or visiting nurse program for hospice care in the home. This is special care for patients during the last three to six months of life. Most often associated with cancer patients, hospice care often involves heavier than normal doses of painkillers to keep their patients from suffering.

When patients are away from home, hospices encourage families to visit any time they wish. Specially trained staff gear the treatment program toward making the patient's last days, weeks, or months as satisfying and painless as possible.

Alzheimer's Disease and Senility

Alzheimer's Disease is a progressive, degenerative disease of the brain. Virtually everyone who contemplates their future is afraid of it, yet only about one percent of Americans actually have it. Even so, Alzheimer's Disease is a tragedy of immense proportions. The disease is concentrated among the elderly, but can strike those under the age of thirty. The American Health Assistance Foundation estimates more than three million Americans may now be suffering from Alzheimer's Disease. Other estimates range from one-and-a-half to four million — including perhaps one out of every four Americans over the age of 85.

The precise number of patients may never be known because a conclusive diagnosis usually requires a physical examination of the brain under a microscope. A brain damaged by Alzheimer's shows characteristic tangles of fibers and degenerated nerve endings, particularly in those areas of the brain used for memory and "intellectual" processes. At present, scientists are striving to better understand the disease, and are searching out possibilities for prevention, diagnosis, and treatment.

Curiously, no two Alzheimer's patients show exactly the same symptoms and behaviors, or deteriorate in the same way. Some people develop trouble walking, driving, or even standing; others don't. Even the rate of deterioration can vary widely. Onset to complete disability may take only a few years in one patient, but as long as fifteen to twenty-five years in another.

In its early stages, Alzheimer's usually shows up as forgetfulness, poor or inappropriate word choices in conversation, and loss of recent memory. However, patients may vividly remember events from their distant childhood, and may have long periods with memory relatively intact. Personality changes can make Mom or Dad seem less spontaneous and lively. He or she may have new difficulties solving simple problems, making decisions, or handling finances, and may also display lapses in social etiquette, such as beginning to undress on the way to the bathroom.

As the disease progresses, sufferers may have more difficulty with their ability to think, to understand or express themselves, to read, and to recognize their own family or their surroundings. They often become easily confused, and may wander away, unable to find their way home. Personality changes may increase. Your parent may become inflexible, grumpy, dissatisfied, argumentative, or physically or verbally abusive, and may be unable to sleep well. Eventually, Alzheimer's patients become chronically fatigued and depressed.

In the later stages, Alzheimer's may rob a person of the ability to dress, swallow, eat, walk, and do the simplest tasks — like using the bathroom — for themselves. Alzheimer's leaves people weakened and more susceptible to pneumonia and other problems, and unlike some other diseases, only gets worse with time.

It's no wonder so many aging Americans, and their adult children, have a real fear of becoming a "vegetable." It's hard to dissuade anyone of the danger, partly because many researchers think Alzheimer's tends to have a genetic link, and partly because no one has yet determined conclusively what causes Alzheimer's or how to treat it. Pharmaceutical companies are eagerly exploring the opportunities for slowing, halting, or reversing the mental deterioration associated with Alzheimer's. However, the search for an effective treatment may take many years.

Despite — or perhaps because of — the large gaps in our understanding of Alzheimer's Disease, it has become a convenient catchword to describe a whole range of symptoms of senility. Many families use "Alzheimer's" as a modern substitute for the vague and more old-fashioned word "senile" to describe an aging parent's incapacity or personality changes, regardless of their cause.

Once "senility" was considered the just reward for a life of alcohol abuse or other excess. Today, we recognize that anyone — regardless of lifestyle — can contract Alzheimer's Disease or other forms of *senile dementia,* which literally means "deprived of mind through old age." Dementia is an organic disease of the brain, not a psychological or emotional problem. About five percent of people over 65 have chronic, irreversible dementia resulting from Alzheimer's and other causes. Another five percent are only moderately impaired.

Even moderate dementia entails more than simple memory loss, so losing the car keys is not necessarily a signal your parent has Alzheimer's. Everyone forgets details, conversations, experiences and information from time to time. Memory can suffer from short-term factors associated with stress, fatigue, illness, distraction, medication and dozens of more major causes, including small strokes, chemical imbalances in the body, depression, thyroid problems, poor nutrition, brain tumors, head injuries and alcoholism. Some of these problems are much more easily treated than others. Research also confirms that, like muscles and other organs, the brain's performance can decline with age.

Aside from memory loss, warning signs of true dementia may include defective judgment, loss of insight or understanding, apathy, and significant personality changes. You may see frequent anger and overreaction to ordinary events, along with rapidly changing moods. Stressful situations may result in weeping, agitation, stubbornness, or even physically striking anyone within reach.

You or your parent's doctor may notice subtle differences in the senility caused by various factors. If your parent suffers a series of small strokes, for example, his or her senile behavior will tend to increase in progressive steps. This is because each stroke or series of strokes destroys a little more of the brain and creates a little more incapacity. But for days, weeks, or months between strokes your Mom or Dad may remain fairly stable. In contrast, an Alzheimer's patient is likely to worsen more steadily.

Caring for Mentally Deteriorated Parents

Whatever the cause of the symptoms, it's important to tell your parent what is happening to them. Most people will recognize the loss of some mental capacity, even if the realization occurs only at some subconscious level and they never openly acknowledge it. Mom or Dad may feel relieved to know a disease is responsible for their mental deficiencies, that they're not just "going crazy" or imagining their problems. It's important for you to emphasize that people with Alzheimer's and other forms of senility can get along for many years with help from others. Confirming that you want to be one of their helpers may cement the bond between you and your aging parent.

However, your parent will also know that the disease will continue to worsen. This can be emotionally traumatic to the sufferer and other family members. Your first instinct may be to keep the news from Mom or Dad, but hiding it doesn't help. You'll find such a secret hard to keep, and the effort can make it more difficult for Mom or Dad to accept the coming decline.

Recognizing the onset of Alzheimer's or other senility is only the first of many long, burdensome and emotionally trying steps. Caring for a senile parent can be a thankless and unending task as they lose contact with reality, and their physical and mental functions deteriorate. Friends and distant relatives may stop offering help because of the practical difficulties and the emotional distress they feel at seeing your Mom or Dad in such bad shape.

But there are ways to mitigate the problems of caring for parents suffering from Alzheimer's or senility. Some of the most important guidelines include:

Take one day at a time. If you worry about how your parent may behave tomorrow, you will only divert some of your strength from what you must accomplish today.

Accept your feelings. Anger, guilt, despair, resentment and other feelings are entirely normal. When you try to repress them, you can do real damage. Make sure you have outlets for expressing your honest feelings to sympathetic and understanding friends and family. Try to express your feelings constructively so they don't build up and tear you apart. Consider joining a caregiver's support group.

Accept your parents as they are. Don't expect too much of them. Put yourself in Mom's or Dad's shoes and realize how distressed you would be not to know the day of the week or to recognize your surroundings. Realize that your parent's irritating behavior results from a mental condition rather than willful intention or bad disposition.

Maintain your sense of humor. After Dan Granger's confinement to a nursing home, his personality shifted from remote and demanding to sweet, dependent and childlike. He became so effusive and warm at times that Estelle, his wife, and Zack, his son, could only laugh to keep from crying. A good laugh at your parent's behavior can sometimes be the family's most therapeutic response.

Of course, it's easier to talk about these guidelines than to follow them in daily practice. Most families suffer terribly when an aging parent develops Alzheimer's Disease. Some research shows that a third of the people caring for Alzheimer's victims are themselves depressed. The day-to-day demands of caring for Alzheimer's patients can become immense. To illustrate, you need only hear about an 86 year-old woman suffering from Alzheimer's whose 60-year-old daughter built up so much frustration and rage over her caregiving responsibilities that she stabbed her own mother to death.

Caregiver Support Groups

If your parent appears to show signs of Alzheimer's or any form of senile dementia, look into an Alzheimer's caregiver support group in your area. These free or low-fee groups are frequently organized at community and religious centers, at hospitals and nursing homes, and at other social service organizations throughout the country. The groups meet regularly and give caregivers an outlet to express their grievances, frustrations, fears, and depression. There's a chance to talk about the little triumphs and joys that also occur in the life of an Alzheimer's patient and his or her family. Joining a group can renew your energy, ease your pain, offer many step-saving tricks and techniques, and otherwise contribute to a significant improvement in your caregiving ability.

Special Considerations

Modern health care presents excruciating dilemmas. The physical deterioration of your parents' bodies may leave them in considerable pain, or may significantly interfere with their ability to function. Specialists can often, but not always, correct their health problems. Some procedures, such as denture fittings or cataract surgery, are fairly routine. Occasionally, your aging parents may be candidates for complicated, dangerous, or expensive treatments. In such situations, the family needs to consider and balance a great many factors, including:

- Your parent's immediate discomfort and long-term health.

- The potential danger and discomfort of specific medical treatment or procedures.

- The likely outcome and recovery time of a particular course of treatment or medical intervention.

- The accessibility and cost of medical care.

- Your parent's ability and willingness to cooperate with treatment.

- The fear and emotional burden on your parent and other family members. Compare the situation if doctors do nothing and allow the problem to continue with the case if they take appropriate medical action.

As we discuss in Chapter 7 (Death-Related Issues), there are also questions regarding how much medical care to provide to terminally ill patients, and under what conditions — if any — to withhold "heroic measures" intended to keep them alive.

You and your parents should decide your answers to these questions and communicate them to your parents' physicians. According to studies, many doctors recognize that talking with their aging patients about when and whether to resuscitate them is unlikely to depress them or do any harm. Nevertheless, most physicians are very cautious about raising this and related questions.

Families often find the question of artificial nourishment to be particularly disturbing. If a parent is no longer able to eat and drink independently, doctors can prolong life by feeding through tubes. Many people feel strongly that withholding this type of treatment is the same as starving a person to death, but others do not believe it is worthwhile to maintain a life in this manner. Whatever you may *think*, you may *feel* very differently when the decision for Mom or Dad must be made.

If your parents don't want to lose control of their own destiny, your family should take firm control of these decisions by executing the appropriate legal documents, including a *health care power of attorney*, which hospitals are increasingly being required to request from patients when first admitted. [See Chapter 7 (Death-Related Issues).]

Some Practical Suggestions

A few simple ideas can greatly improve your parents' safety and comfort:

- Encourage your parents to get regular medical checkups. It is possible to detect and reverse certain conditions that, left untreated, can cause serious damage and disability. Persevere, because many older people are reluctant to call doctors or go for examinations and can suffer as a result of this old-fashioned idea.

- Ask all their doctors to give written, clearly legible instructions with every prescription and treatment plan your parents must follow. Your parents may not remember all the details of verbal directions regarding what to do and when to do it, particularly if they are not feeling well. If the doctor balks, encourage your parents to find someone more concerned about their well-being.

- Encourage your parents to check with their doctor about a preventive pneumonia vaccine and/or a flu vaccine.

- Inactive people are particularly prone to pneumonia. Be alert for symptoms, such as fever and headache, malaise, chills and cough. Shaking chills, temperatures to 105 degrees, rapid breathing and coughing may be symptoms of the more dangerous *bacterial* pneumonia. Don't let your parents wait to obtain treatment for either one.

- Heart attacks can masquerade as indigestion, back pain, or pressure in the chest. Watch for severe sweating and signs of pain down the arm. Only about a third of heart attack victims have the classic chest pain. If you're concerned, immediately take Mom or Dad to the emergency room. Don't wait for damage to occur.

- Be alert for foul-smelling breath, or pains in the jaw or gum, which can indicate your parents are having tooth problems. Bad teeth can prevent your parents from eating enough for good health. Tooth loss can limit their ability to eat and, coupled with the natural loss of taste sensations, can lead to loss of weight and strength.

- Encourage your parents to replace their lost teeth with well-fitted dentures. This helps them maintain good nutrition and eating habits. If they won't wear dentures, they should adjust their diet to emphasize soft foods and nourishing liquids.

- Help your parents obtain proper nutrition in case they become housebound for any reason, such as sudden illness or bad weather. Leave them a supply of instant milk, for example, and provide enough sandwiches in the freezer for several meals.

- People suffering from urinary problems may make frequent nighttime dashes to the bathroom. Make sure the path is clear and eliminate any loose rugs on which they can slip or other safety hazards. Adult diapers as well as rubber sheets on the bed can eliminate much of the expense and embarrassment associated with incontinence.

- Get your parents a fever thermometer with large numbers they can easily read. One simple device is a "fever strip" they can place on the forehead to get a reading.

- Keep your parents away from grandchildren with chicken pox. Exposure can give them *zoster* (formerly called *shingles*).

- If your parents are suffering from Alzheimer's Disease, you may want to place a large clock and calendar where they can see it, label frequently used doors and drawers, and install double-cylinder locks on exit doors to help prevent wandering.

- If your parent develops Alzheimer's or dementia of any sort, consider having them wear a bracelet with their name, address and phone number. At the least, place a card with identifying information in their wallet or purse. Should Mom or Dad wander away, the information will allow police or anyone who tries to help to more easily contact you or bring them back home.

- Review the suggestions given earlier in this chapter involving handling of medications.

CHAPTER 5

EMOTIONAL ISSUES

Housing, financial matters and health are all critical concerns when helping your parents maintain a good quality of life. But no less important are the emotional issues that come up during this time of stress and change.

Parents' Emotions

Even if they are in the best of physical and mental health, your aging parents can face severe bouts of loneliness, depression, fear and anger. These emotions can seriously disrupt a person's life and relationships at any time. When your parents are also facing age-related disabilities and deteriorating health, the added burden of these emotions can be too much to bear. Your parents' emotional turmoil can put other members of the family through significant emotional changes, with unexpected effects on young children, elderly aunts and uncles, or anyone who feels a strong tie to those in need.

Many people can learn to moderate their emotional reactions to parents who begin needing help. But it's usually impossible to eliminate all the feeling, and trying would probably do more harm than good. A far more reasonable goal is to understand the interpersonal process causing the emotional distress, to recognize that others have had similar experiences, and to "weather the storm" until the situation improves. It also helps to talk with others, to share feelings and to express your emotions away from the family, where outbursts will do less harm and cause fewer repercussions.

Loneliness

Loneliness is unfortunately one of the hallmarks of aging. In too many families, symptoms of old age tend to isolate parents from familiar friends, activities and surroundings. From their point of view, they may suddenly be driven from their long-time home and neighborhood, stricken with illness or immobilized, and prevented from participating in life as they once did. They may be confined in strange and impersonal hospital rooms for days or weeks, or in nursing homes for years — perhaps against their will. The normal result of these or any other isolating changes is a feeling of loneliness.

If your parents are suddenly housebound, you may be able to ward off their loneliness — at least in the short term — by visiting more often and by encouraging others to visit.

As Glenda Somerset's arthritis became very severe, she was virtually imprisoned in her house and almost entirely cut off from her previously active lifestyle. But Cindy, one of her daughters, took pains to visit for an hour or two at least three times a week. She and her husband, Mort, often brought one of Glenda's sisters, who lived in the same town. They also encouraged Glenda to keep in touch with her friends regularly by telephone and to invite them in for drinks or a few hours of cards. Some of these evenings, Cindy and Mort helped out, allowing Glenda more time with her friends. As a result of these efforts, Glenda never felt the severe loneliness that plagues so many seniors. She was grateful to Cindy and Mort, who — though hard pressed to find time for Glenda amid their own daily pressures and child-rearing respon- sibilities — were happy they could make such a big difference in her quality of life.

Loneliness can also become a factor when your parents move to a new home. They will probably take several months, or longer, to make new friends. Most people find old friends hard to leave and new relation- ships somewhat uncomfortable to start. Your parents' move can also exaggerate the shyness they may ordinari- ly feel when thrown together with strangers. Also, they simply may not *want* to form friendships with people in retirement communities or nursing homes. This is a more perverse problem to overcome.

If your parents are not developing relationships as quickly as you think they normally would, you may want to try making friends and acquaintances there yourself and serving as something of a bridge from the new com- munity into your parents' lives. Usually, the loneliness problem gets better as time passes.

Loneliness can have a much more devastating effect when your parent is unwilling to accept change. A parent who feels "imprisoned" by events or by unloving relatives — as a surprising number of aging parents do — often experiences a particularly painful form of loneliness.

The most trying cause of loneliness your parents may need to overcome is the adjustment to age-related infir- mities. They may see every restriction on movement, every limitation of their range of action as a rejection or a loss of rights and privileges. Their feelings of independence and self-control can quickly evaporate. A move to a nursing home is often the most severe trial. Most people will normally take a while to adjust, yet they will ultimately accept that they need constant supervision, whether their problem is forgetfulness, loss of bladder or bowel control, a medical problem that requires monitoring, or anything else. However, some parents never fully adjust.

When a parent is confined to a hospital or nursing home, other family members commonly feel their own share of loneliness. The spouse is often hardest hit, particularly if the pair have been together most of their lives. Sometimes, however, the loneliness a spouse feels is actually an emotional substitute for a gnawing fear that their loved one is about to die, and that they will soon follow. After your parent has lost a spouse or a close family member, he or she will probably feel at least some degree of loneliness, conceivably forever.

Adult children and grandchildren can also feel lonely when illness or age-related disability strikes a loved one. Grandchildren feel lonely when Grandma or Grandpa can no longer play with them or visit as frequently as before. Holiday celebrations feel different, offering unmistakable evidence of life's major changes. For adult children, the loneliness grows out of identifying with their parent, feeling what their parents are feeling, and not liking the experience.

There is no real antidote for loneliness, though the passage of time and the company of loved ones helps immeasurably. Don't expect overnight adjustments. Give your parent plenty of time and as much attention as you can, but realize that round-the-clock visiting is impossible. Even if you could be there all the time, your presence would not erase every bit of loneliness. Some will remain until your parent becomes familiar with his or her new surroundings and feels a part of it.

As a rule, plan to spend extra time with your Mom or Dad for the first week or two in their new home. Keep visiting, even if they don't seem to know you or appreciate your presence. Share some meals with them. Pass the time in simple conversation, talking about family, friends, or whatever interests them. Help them get settled and arrange furniture to their liking. Decorate the room with photographs of family members and a calendar with birthdays and other celebrations boldly marked on it. Bring flowers from home.

If they're confined to a hospital for a short-term problem, you may be able to visit every day until they leave. If they move into retirement housing or a nursing home, you can start by visiting fairly often, then taper off over a period of a week or two. Schedule your regular visits with enough time between them so your parent can begin to make his or her own relationships, and won't depend too heavily on your continual presence.

Also, during your visits make sure Mom or Dad has opportunities for contact with others. Sit or stroll in the common areas where others can see your parent and introduce themselves. When you leave, don't always escort your parent to a private area. Consider leaving him or her with a group of people, or at least nearby. The others may strike up a conversation, or include them in the group. The more you help your Mom or Dad get out and about, the more quickly they will get acclimated and shed some of their loneliness. But be careful not to push so hard you contribute to your parent's feeling of power-lessness.

Depression

Depression is one of the most common reactions to advancing age. According to some experts, as many as fifteen percent of Americans over the age of 65 suffer from a clinically significant degree of depression. They may express their depression as apathy, as withdrawal from social activities, or as a negative attitude to events around them. Most often, they won't recognize or admit their own depression. Instead, they'll steadily complain of aches and pains, bad treatment by others, insomnia, or loss of appetite.

Melancholy feelings or early depression in older people can rob them of their zest for life. This, in turn, makes them less interested in taking good care of themselves. They give up and fall into a deeper depression that becomes a spiral leading downward to apathy and quite possibly death.

A parent's depression isn't always caused by a psychological illness. It can be a side effect of prescribed medications. Sometimes a single drug causes depression. However, most doctors are becoming more aware of the danger and make at least some effort to monitor their older patients for this. In other cases, a certain combination of several drugs is the hidden and unsuspected cause of a parent's heavy depression. Families rarely understand that helpful drugs prescribed for purely physical problems can lead to such strong emotional reactions. A doctor prescribing one of the known depressive drugs might recognize the potential for a problem, but the chances of anticipating a depressive reaction to medication remain quite slim unless the physician considers all the drugs, vitamins and other preparations your parent is taking. To help your parents' doctors avoid inducing emotional side effects, give them a list of all these substances before they prescribe for Mom or Dad. In addition, take the precaution of clearing any medication changes ordered by one doctor for Mom or Dad with all the other doctors as well.

You may want to ask a pharmacist or pharmacologist for help. They can consult references and computer programs to evaluate possible interactions among many substances. Remember why they are prescription drugs — they have the potential to be dangerous. So be sure to consider this possible cause of your parent's depression. In many cases, a simple change in medication has lifted the depression in a matter of days.

The Keyes family learned this first-hand. Jerry, well over 70, was in fairly good health when his doctor changed his blood pressure medication. Soon after, Jerry became depressed and fatigued, lost weight, and looked ill. Eventually, his son, Frank, and his daughter-in-law, Kate, convinced Jerry to allow his doctor to hospitalize him for tests. While in the hospital, Jerry was taken off all medication. Within a few days his depression disappeared. He regained his healthy appearance and his appetite, and looked forward to leaving the hospital and playing with his grandsons. His doctors prescribed a different regimen of medication, with smaller doses. Within a month, Jerry regained his former health, and has stayed well and happy for more than a year.

Aside from medication and mental illness, aging parents may fall into depression for the same reason as anyone else: they feel an acute sense of loss. For most older people, loss is a frequent experience of daily life. They lose a measure of financial security every time inflation cuts their purchasing power. They lose some of their physical and mental capacities, and some of their independence. They lose most of the external signposts that define their identity: a job title, a family role as a provider or homemaker, and influence within a social group or organization. They also lose friends and acquaintances who die.

While some doctors prescribe mild medication for depression, exposure to new and interesting people, events, experiences and opportunities can be the best treatment for depression caused by something other than drugs or illness. You can sometimes help clear away depression if you take your parent on excursions to new places, or on daily errands, and if you plan activities with Mom or Dad. Involve the family and some of your parent's new acquaintances. Though it may help, don't be naive and think a single experience, such as a meeting of a senior social group, will boost your parent out of a depression and get him or her dancing. Benefits are more likely to flow from steady encouragement to participate in many different activities. Each activity or event can help open the door to a positive difference in outlook. However, your parent must be willing to walk through it.

For a while, your parent's depression may feed on itself and linger. But with proper support — and where needed, medical supervision and treatment — most elderly people can recover from depression and regain their emotional equilibrium. If none of this works and your parent's doctor has ruled out physical causes and side effects from medication, you should consult a psychiatrist or other mental health professional who specializes in geriatrics. Don't give up because of your parent's age or possible prejudices against psychiatry. Thousands of older people have been helped out of their depression. You may have to provide a great deal of support to get your parent started in treatment. In extreme cases, potent medications or electroconvulsive therapy can greatly reduce depression.

Fear

For many people, old age is a time of relentless fear: fear of death, their own and those of friends and loved ones; fear of their growing incapacity; fear of illness and pain. For some, there are other fears, equally real: poverty, loss of independence, being deserted or being confined to an "old-age home." These feelings tend to persist, particularly when based on all-too-real possibilities.

To understand the origins of these fears, imagine yourself in your parent's shoes. How would you feel if your eyesight or hearing were failing? As you grew weaker and more susceptible to illness and injury, wouldn't you grow fearful of ordinary experiences, like being caught in bad weather or climbing or descending steep staircases?

Fear makes sense two ways: It's an older person's reasonable reaction to the dangers of everyday life. It's also a natural expression of their underlying anticipation of death. When we are young, it's normal to feel invincible and immortal. As we grow older, though, many of us feel our grip on life begin to weaken. We fear losing that grip. It's wrong to deny this feeling, or to belittle your parent for expressing this fear to you.

As your parents continue to weaken and suffer from health problems, it's perfectly understandable for the fear of death to surface. Although they may express it as fear of the dark, fear of being mugged, or fear of anything else, fear of death may become a major emotional force in their approach to daily life.

Since death is inevitable, there's little you can do to allay your parents' fear. However, you can and should take reasonable steps against any of the practical matters they fear. For example, you can help them upgrade their door and window locks or take other security measures in their home. You can fight their fear of sudden illness by helping them get regular medical check-ups. You can get professionals to devise a good financial plan so they can push fear of poverty into the background.

Recognize that after you help them eliminate one danger, your parents may easily find something else to fear. Nevertheless, it is useful to take steps to eliminate the fears one by one. This changes the topic of complaints as fears shift from one source to another. More important, should misfortune befall your parents, you'll know you helped them take all reasonable precautions, and thus you may place less blame on yourself.

Anger and Resentment

Anger and resentment are other expressions of worry about incapacity, pain and death. Aging parents' dispositions can rapidly change from basically happy to bitter and mean, a transition which understandably begins to poison their relationships.

One common source of resentment in parents is their jealousy and regret over their inability to care for themselves, and their lack of freedom and independence. Although basically happy and content, 78-year-old Emilio Gonzalez felt a strong resentment toward his son, Jose. Every time the younger man understood a financial opportunity and made a decision for him, or drove his father or his mother, Blanca, to a doctor's appointment because they could no longer drive themselves, Emilio expressed his resentment in muttered insults that irritated everyone in the family.

There's no easy way to handle a parent who turns angry or resentful. Mom or Dad may overreact to the mailman delivering late, the bus driver hitting potholes in the street, the store clerk working too slow, or the waitress who brings a cold meal. They may resent your offers of help, and your ability to deliver it. Solving all these problems — itself an impossible and thankless task — wouldn't do much to alleviate your parent's feelings. They'd simply switch targets and start lambasting the next available person, place, or thing.

In reality, most older people who turn angry or resentful seem to be furious at life for forcing them to grow old and suffer. They're angry at themselves, too, for letting it happen. You may try to be sweet, attentive and warm, but there's little chance you can defuse such deep-seated emotion. Many aging parents don't want to be soothed, and purposely direct their anger and resentment to hurt loved ones, or those trying hardest to help them.

In the Putnam family, for example, Lewis and Rhonda waited more than two hours for their first appointment with their new geriatrician. During the office visit, the elderly couple were extremely nice and friendly to the young doctor. However, as soon as they got in the car for the ride home, they lashed out at their son, Scott, and his wife, Susan. They recited a whole litany of errors, omissions, bad manners and just plain insensitive behavior that Scott and Susan had supposedly committed over the past few weeks. Shaken, the younger couple said nothing and listened to their aging parents for over twenty minutes. Later, Susan and Scott had a brief argument of their own, and their young children walked around with their heads down for a few days. Relations between Susan and her in-laws were severely strained for several weeks.

It took a social worker interviewing all four of the Putnams to recognize that Lewis and Rhonda were really dumping their anger at the young doctor on their adult children. They were resentful about growing old, and becoming so helpless and needy of assistance. Armed with this insight, Susan and Scott eventually learned not to take their parents' outbursts so personally. It still hurts, of course, but they take comfort from realizing their parents are not truly angry with them, and are simply using a comfortable and safe environment to express their feelings toward others. Lately, Susan and Scott have been gently, calmly, and patiently pointing out their parents' anger and resentment whenever it comes up. They ask questions such as: "Are you angry with the doctor or with me?" and "Are you really resentful about my other commitments, or are you feeling badly about something else?"

In the Gonzalez family, Emilio's personality changed dramatically in the years after he began suffering circulation problems that kept him in bed or a wheelchair most of the time. He had been a warm, gentle father and husband. But now he unveiled a violent temper. His adult children, Maria, Jose and Manuel, did everything they could to please him, but the old man had only harsh words for them, for his doctors, and for Carlos and Florentina, his own brother and sister. It was only in the last hours before he died that he forgave his family for everything he imagined they had done to hurt him in the past few years, and he apologized for treating them so badly.

The best response to anger is often to let it blow right through you. When your father yells at you for ignoring him or leaving him in a nursing home, you might understand he's really angry at himself for becoming old and incapacitated. When your mother berates you for going out to work when you should be staying home and tending to your family, you might realize she's really lashing out at her own problems and pains. Don't hold your breath and expect their anger to dissipate. Many older people who become angry near the end of their lives don't easily give it up. Some people enjoy the feeling of anger and the adrenalin rush it brings, and use it to avoid feeling bad about their present circumstances. Many older people express fear of death as anger. Others use anger to release tension and anxiety. For whatever reasons, your parents may stubbornly hang onto this way of expressing themselves.

Most important, don't let your parent's anger make you feel guilty about the pain they say you have caused, the responsibilities they say you have ignored, or the damage they say you have done. Whatever the source, your parent's anger is a process. The *anger itself* is often the message. The content of *what they say* may be far less important, and may even be untrue.

Of course, you should be careful in expressing these insights. Even if they apply, your parent won't be receptive. Nevertheless, understanding what causes your parent's anger may bring you some comfort and can help you accept his or her outbursts without getting angry in return.

You may want to try exploring your parent's feelings underneath his or her outward anger. This is a delicate business. Don't expect to cure your parent of angry feelings without undergoing a long, complex and uncomfortable process of growth and honest sharing. In some cases, you may do Mom or Dad the most good by encouraging them to seek help from a professional.

Life After Death of a Spouse

If life were a novel, loving spouses would die within a very short time of each other. Although this happens occasionally, in most families one spouse (or long-term companion) continues to live on — sometimes seemingly against his or her will. Your parent must face responsibilities, daily routines, friends and family, pleasures and pains all without the companionship, help, guidance and support of a long-term life partner.

After the death of a spouse, life changes drastically. However, the changes are significantly different for men and women of older generations.

For men, the loss of a wife generally means assuming more responsibilities for daily chores, meals, housework and social planning. Without women, men can sometimes have trouble making new friends, keeping busy, and generally maintaining their home and their happiness. Older men can spend much of their time moping around the house, failing to develop new activities and sources of happiness, and gradually falling into depression. This may continue for years, or until they develop a relationship with another woman.

However, men who have lost their wives are frequently sought out by their friends and included in social activities. Since there are far fewer widowers than widows (one-fifth or one-sixth as many over age 65, because women generally outlive men), and since women tend to be very solicitous of others, after his wife's death a single man often finds himself the center of attention and social activity within his group.

For women, the loss of a husband often forces them to start handling financial affairs and household repairs, and take greater responsibility for making major decisions. Given the structure of Social Security and other retirement plans, widows may have to survive on lower incomes than widowers of comparable ages. Some widows see less of their married friends; they may feel uncomfortable around other men without having a man of their own, or married women may feel threatened by them, afraid the widows may steal their husbands. Nevertheless, widows can survive quite well without a man. They frequently develop active social lives — traveling, playing cards, taking classes, volunteering, and keeping far busier than they did when their husbands were alive.

Women generally seem to be more aware than men of the possibility of losing their spouse. Many aging women give a lot of thought to the future, and devote much of their energy to preserving their husbands' health. Men who outlive their wives generally seem less prepared, often suffering more emotional shock and taking longer to recover.

In addition to the expected grief and mourning, there can be physical symptoms, too: loss of weight, sudden graying or other signs of aging, sleepless nights and a general irritability. For a surviving spouse, depression — separate from grief and mourning — is common. The death of a spouse can feel like an amputation: a part of one's self is gone. Although old age is usually character-ized by the loss of capabilities, material possessions and friends, the death of a spouse is often the most devastat-ing loss of all — requiring quite a long time to get back on an even keel.

Sometimes, however, the surviving parent shows an opposite reaction: A sense of freedom and lightness of spirit that may seem completely inappropriate to some family members. It occurs most often when the deceased was a long-time burden to the surviving spouse, or a harsh, demanding and controlling person. Occasionally, this reaction appears in completely unexpected situa-tions. It may just be masking the surviving parent's real feelings.

One thing is certain, the time following the death of a spouse is a highly unstable period. After the initial shock and dislocation, the survivor struggles to find a new lifestyle. One month your widowed father may be a recluse disinterested in social activities, and the next month he is chatting amiably alongside a swimming pool or playing checkers regularly. Or your widowed mother may take up volunteer work, then drop everything for a

cruise or a vacation in the sun. After a while, your aging
parent will tend to settle into a more or less comfortable
routine. He or she will learn to handle the late spouse's
chores and will become better adjusted to the loss. Life
may never again be as good as it once was, but it will
probably become more endurable.

Remarriage and New Relationships

Because most people deeply desire the companionship and security of a relationship, widows and widowers
sometimes pair up rather quickly after losing a spouse.
Try not to be shocked or offended by a new romance or
relationship, which may include hugging, kissing, or
sexual activity. Remember, your surviving parent may be
feeling very lonely and isolated. He or she may have spent
years caring for a seriously debilitated and dependent
spouse, enduring hardship and unhappiness that now
deserves some release. A new partner can bring your
parent a more active social life, opportunities for travel,
emotional bonding and personal fulfillment. There may
be favorable financial considerations. If Mom or Dad can
gain some pleasure and happiness from a new romance
with someone they've known or have recently met, why
should they delay?

It's wise, though, to urge some caution — the same
caution you would urge on anyone at any age entering a
new relationship. There are dangers from opportunists
and charlatans. "Confidence men" make their living by
marrying one widow after another and taking as much
money from each one as they can; some older women
make a practice of befriending widowers and encouraging
them to lavish jewelry, travel, cars, stocks and other
assets on them. Even when intentions are entirely honor-

able, there are dangers from moving into a new relationship too fast, including the danger of sexually transmitted diseases.

In the Price family, for example, Lillian grieved deeply when her husband of forty-five years suddenly passed away. She was terribly lonely and distraught for nearly a year. Then she met Ted, a vigorous 70 year-old man who had lost his wife a few years earlier. The two hit it off immediately and began spending much of their time together. Lillian's son, Frank, was happy for his mother, and didn't object when she announced that Ted was going to move into her apartment and share the expenses.

Frank, Lillian and Ted got along beautifully for more than six months. But then Lillian began to tire of Ted's personal habits, and the tasteless jokes he told her friends and family. After several more months, she was sure she wanted Ted to move out. However, he had nowhere to go. Meanwhile, Lillian had grown used to his gifts, as well as his monthly contributions for rent, food, entertainment and other expenses. The family suffered for another six months before Ted finally agreed to get his own apartment. Frank feels strongly that if Ted had not moved in with his mother, or if Lillian had moved in with Ted, the logistics would have allowed the two to "break up" much more easily and quickly.

Before your parent makes a serious commitment to a new romance or other relationship, encourage him or her to consider a number of important factors:

- The pros and cons of committing to an exclusive relationship without first spending a fair amount of time together.

- The pros and cons of living together rather than marrying, at least for a trial period. Note any financial consequences of remarrying, because some pensions or retirement benefits may be irrevocably lost. There may also be some consequences for passing the estate of the deceased to the spouse and/or the children, particularly in states with community property laws. Yet living together without marriage can lead to gossip, guilt feelings and enormous pressures on an otherwise solid relationship. This may be especially true for people of older generations.

• His or her willingness to accept responsibility for the new partner, should illness, injury, or other debilitating problems strike.

• His or her understanding of the financial arrangements. They should make clear to each other (not necessarily to you) the resources each brings to the relationship, how they will share their income and expenses, and any implications their relationship may hold for the estates they will leave behind. Encourage your parents to consult an attorney and consider signing a formal prenuptial or "palimony" agreement.

Although your parent should consider all these practical matters, a new relationship may have emotional significance which outweighs any of the practical matters.

Try to help others in the family see this side of the situation. Sometimes, family members resent a parent's new relationship, feeling it betrays the memory of the deceased spouse. Some may have a hard time welcoming a new member to the family; others might worry about losing their share of any inheritance.

Even thinking about the possibility of Mom or Dad in a new romance or relationship can create emotional conflict within the family. It's important to share your feelings with your parent, as well as with other family members. Be careful here: Don't force your aging parent to choose between family concerns and his or her own happiness. Try to put yourself in a "parenting" frame of mind. You want your children to be happy and secure in a warm, loving relationship. You should have the same goals for your aging parent. It's best if you can feel delighted that Mom or Dad is capable of finding and maintaining a good relationship despite advancing age.

Relationships Between Parents and Adult Children

One change that takes place when you begin parenting your aging parents is the readjustment of your relationship. You began life dependent on them. As you grew up, you may have pulled away, or moved closer to being equals and friends. Either way, you grew to be as independent as they were. However, as your parents continue to age and you take a greater role in maintaining their quality of life, they tend to become more dependent on you.

Expect to be swept by a series of emotional storms as this change takes place. You'll alternate between feelings of childishness and parenthood. At times you'll feel overwhelmed, scared, or resentful that you have so much control over their lives. Other times, you'll feel you have no control at all. You can't avoid these feelings, so you might as well let them wash over you.

Resist any impulse to judge yourself or your parents. Don't expect to be patient and loving toward your parents all the time. Blow-ups, disagreements and bad feelings are inevitable in almost every family; under stress, they occur quite frequently in some. Having "unloving" feelings toward your parents doesn't mean you don't love them or you're a bad person. After all, you're under pressure in a demanding situation that's changing rapidly. Under these stressful conditions, no one with responsibility for their aging parents can avoid occasional emotional backlash.

Handle your feelings in a fair and open manner. Accept them, express them, and try to understand their origins. But be careful. Although accepting and expressing your feelings is beneficial, this doesn't give you carte blanche to explode at your aging parents. It may momentarily feel good to vent your feelings quickly and directly at others, but your parents are an unfair target. It's healthier for all concerned if you discharge your feelings through strenuous exercise, engrossing activity, or during time you purposely spend away from your parents and responsibilities to them. You might also discuss your feelings with a brother or sister to whom you feel close, or with others you trust who are in a position to know, to understand, or to help. Therapy or support groups can be useful for all caregivers, and especially those with hard-to-handle feelings.

A Balanced Approach to Caregiving

In many families, adult children trying to care for their aging parents become unforgiving taskmasters. Everyone must tiptoe when Grandpa is resting. Family members must bake his favorite cookies, mend his clothes and visit every week. The adult children themselves must make careful, prudent, perfect decisions for their aging parents on everything from housing and finances to diet and social activities. This approach is almost always a terrible mistake.

When you impose too many responsibilities or too high a standard on yourself, you set yourself up for failure, heartache and a host of emotional problems. It doesn't make sense to neglect your own children, your job, or your other family, social and financial responsibilities to spend all your time and energy caring for aging parents. It's much more reasonable to allocate your energies fairly. Do what you can for your parents and be happy about it. Don't punish yourself because you can't do more.

A good rule of thumb is to follow your instincts. If you have a strong urge to be with your children, rather than with your parents, then do it. If you feel you need a break from visiting your parents , or they're able to do more for themselves than they have been doing, give up some of the responsibility you've been carrying. Try taking a short vacation, or at least skip part of your routine for a short while. Inside most of us is someone with very sound judgment. If you find this inner voice and listen to its advice, you'll make far fewer mistakes.

Another important strategy is to contribute to your parents' well-being from your strengths rather than your weaknesses. Your parents may require an entire range of social, financial, medical and psychological services, yet you're probably not qualified to provide them all personally. If you understand their financial options, it may make sense for you to handle this responsibility on your own. If you're familiar with local organizations, you might try to get them involved in activities they would enjoy. If you know about home repair, you might widen their doorways and install the handrails they need. But just as you would take them to a doctor for medical problems, consider using experts and specialists for some or all of the problem areas in which you're not particularly adept — such as housing, finance, social services, or physical rehabilitation. Do the best for your parents by getting them the best help, rather than by trying on your own to give them all the help they need.

Overall, don't expect to be the perfect son or daughter. Be content with trying hard and making a long-term effort. It's almost inevitable you'll make mistakes. Don't browbeat yourself. It's far better to learn from your mistakes and try to avoid making the same ones twice.

Remember, you may have to continue your caregiving for many years. Don't expend your energy in a flurry of activity for the first few months, only to run out of steam and end up so frustrated and exhausted you leave your parents to their own devices. Set realistic goals you can sustain as long as necessary.

It's important to leave room in your relationship for the opportunities you'll need to take care of your own physical and mental health, as well as your spouse and children, your work, your friends, your hobbies and interests, and whatever else makes your life worthwhile. If you neglect these wellsprings of happiness and energy, you'll shortchange both yourself and your parents who need you.

Adult Children's Feelings

Adult children who try to help their parents maintain a good quality of life in their declining years often encounter emotions similar to those their parents feel — for different reasons.

Controlling Your Own Guilt

Guilt has been the subject of so many comedy routines and cultural stereotypes that we forget guilt is both natural and normal. Your feelings of guilt are a personal signal you have done something — or are about to do something — you feel is wrong.

If you're sitting with your sick mother one day, and you decide to leave her alone for an hour to run an errand, you may well feel guilty while you are away. Next time, you'll be more inclined to find someone to stay with your mother, or you'll run the errand another day. Similarly, if you're overseeing your father's retirement fund, and you feel guilty that you left most of the money in bonds when it should have been in a money market account, your guilt may be telling you that you're paying too little attention to these important financial matters.

The biggest problem with guilt is that we sometimes feel guilty without good reason. For example, Betty (Gladstone) felt guilty every time she went out to dinner with her husband, George. She kept thinking it was "wrong" not to invite her mother, Willa, who regularly mentioned how bored and lonely she was. But Betty and George preferred spicy Indian food that Willa would be unable to eat. Nor would Betty's mother have been good company for the intimate conversations and practical discussions Betty and George carried on during these dinners. Betty had a problem with guilt, because she felt she was doing something "wrong" when she was actually doing something perfectly "right."

Some people try to rid themselves of guilt by taking pains never to do anything that makes them feel guilty. This can be very difficult, since no one operates in a vacuum. One day Cindy (Somerset) made plans to spend a few hours with her son, but her mother, Glenda, called and asked to be taken shopping. No matter what Cindy decided to do, she was bound to feel guilty. If your sense of guilt is like Cindy's, easily aroused, you can drive yourself crazy trying to avoid feeling any guilt at all.

A better approach would be to use your judgment consistently to do the "right" thing, while resigning yourself to feeling a certain amount of guilt regardless of how well you behave. If you need reassurance about your judgments, check with friends and family regarding what you want to do in difficult situations. Using good judgment to fight excessive guilt feelings is not a foolproof remedy. But short of intensive psychotherapy and a lot of good luck in avoiding guilt, it can be very effective.

Sadness Among Family Members

Sadness is one of the most common emotions that confronts a family with aging parents who need help. Parents feel sad about their losses: lost friends and loved ones, lost mobility and health, lost income and assets, lost years and opportunities, lost self-esteem, and more. Their brothers and sisters share some of these same feelings. Adult children feel sad about their parents' decline. They may also feel sad about the specific changes they make in their own lives while trying to care for their aging parents.

Grandchildren may also feel sadness. They don't like to see Grandma and Grandpa in trouble. A few recognize the sadness in their own parents and respond sympathetically. What's more, the pressures on their parents may alter their lives enough so they feel sad about the changes, or about past pleasures and opportunities no longer available to them. The fun of playing catch with Grandpa or eating Grandma's cakes disappears when one or both of them becomes incapacitated. The family delays its trip to Disney World or the Grand Canyon because of Grandpa's illness, or a father gives up coaching his son's baseball team to spend more time with Grandma.

There's little to do about such occasional and inevitable sadness. Family members can nevertheless try
to raise their spirits. For example, Frank Keyes goes
fishing for a few days, or shops with his wife for a few
hours, to forget his troubles and enjoy himself for a while.
You may get some pleasure at a local museum or a ball
game, washing the car or planting a garden, taking a walk
or organizing a family picnic.

When sadness lingers too long, it's a good idea to go
back to basics. Think back to your favorite activities when
you were younger. Doing them again will probably give
you an emotional lift. If you can't handle those youthful
activities you loved, try simple modifications and up-
dates. For example, Sandra Johnson can't swim in the
ocean as she once did, but still enjoys floating in the pool
at the Community Center. Brent Warmont and his wife
have as much fun dancing to slow, less demanding music
as they had at the dances when they were in high school.

Anger and Resentment in Families

Anger and resentment are probably two of the least
talked about, yet most common emotions in families
caring for aging parents. There are certainly many good,
warm, enjoyable parts of the process. There are also many
pressures, difficult decisions, considerable expenses, uncomfortable situations and tremendous changes. The
usual result: a huge reservoir of anger and resentment.
Adult children frequently resent both their parent's *need*
for assistance and their *resistance* to accepting offers of
help.

Resentment can also be a mask for other emotions,
including anger, sadness and guilt. The same situations
and concerns can generate all these feelings, which can
and do coexist. The main question, then, is not whether

people in the family will feel any anger or resentment. They will. It's more relevant to ask "At whom will they direct it?"

Scott and Susan Putnam came to understand that his parents, Lewis and Rhonda, routinely expressed at them the anger they felt toward others. But they didn't recognize so readily that Scott was prone to the same problem. The younger couple went through several weeks barely speaking to each other, and later ruined a weekend alone in the mountains by fighting over what Scott had cooked for dinner the previous Wednesday. It wasn't until they had a serious argument the day after Lewis and Rhonda had caused him to miss an important business meeting, however, that Scott recognized much of his fighting with Susan resulted from misdirected resentment and anger he felt toward his parents.

A common source of anger and resentment is the impact caring for your parents has on other aspects of your life. You can easily find yourself with less time for your own family, your work, your hobbies and just plain relaxation. You may have less money as well. Caring for parents can interfere with your privacy, disrupt your sleep, confuse your relationships, saddle you with responsibility and worries you probably don't need and generally reduce your freedom at a time in your life when your responsibilities toward your children may finally be lessening. Such interference and intrusions will almost certainly make you angry and resentful at one time or another.

Many adult children have difficulty acknowledging their own anger and resentment toward aging parents. Yet, when you get a call from your parents in the middle of a busy work day, it's appropriate to feel a little angry and resentful about being pulled away from other important responsibilities. When Mom and Dad suddenly become part of a special dinner or celebration you planned with friends, you can expect a certain amount of anger or resentment to well up at their intrusion. You may even resent family members who don't thank you effusively enough for all you do to help.

Pretending you're not sad or angry or resentful won't work. Keeping your feelings bottled up can make you feel worse in the long run. Talk to trusted friends and family about your cares and problems. Support groups for caregivers may also prove helpful. None of this will eliminate your problems, but may lighten your burden for a while, give you the strength to carry on, or help you find a way to reduce the impact of the source of your emotion.

Frustration

Expect to feel frustrated at least some of the time you're helping your parents. It's the natural human reaction when we don't seem to be making any progress, or when things get worse despite our best efforts. Since slow progress or no progress — and in fact decline — are hallmarks of caring for aging parents, you can expect to deal with a lot of frustration for a long while.

Frustration can be generated by virtually any situation, or by almost anyone. Your parents' refusal to move to an apartment where their lives would be easier is almost certain to frustrate you. When you keep pushing for the move, despite their open resistance, they probably feel frustrated with you.

You'll also find plenty of frustration in dealing with doctors, insurance companies, social workers and therapists, government bureaucracies and even other members of your family. Caring for aging parents usually involves more tedium than anyone imagines. There are a thousand tiny details to oversee, coordinate, consider and select. Yet there are few guidelines or signposts to tell you if you're making life better or worse for your parents.

You'll probably become most frustrated by situations that don't allow easy solutions. For example, as your parents weaken and lose capabilities, you'll find there's no way to restore their faculties, their strength, or their previous lifestyle. You'll become frustrated because there's no "best" solution to most of their problems. Each option has good points and bad points to weigh and balance.

There's no easy way to handle frustration. Of course, you'll want to recognize frustration as an inevitable fact of life, and think about where it comes from. Since frustration is a pent-up drive to accomplish something, you can often reduce its power through physical activity. Anything from chopping wood or cleaning out a closet to a fast game of racquetball or a relaxing round of golf can go a long way toward defusing the frustration time bomb.

It's also helpful to fight frustration by celebrating every little change for the better. If you modify a toilet or bath so your parent can use it a little more conveniently, that's progress. If your Mom, who's suffering from Alzheimer's, gives you a smile as she remembers a moment from an earlier time, relish it. Take as much pleasure as you can from these small triumphs. You may wait a while before you find something else to celebrate.

People are complex, and caregiving relationships between adult children and their parents can reflect virtually all of this complexity, and more. So don't expect too much. Appreciate the good you're attempting, and congratulate yourself for any improvements you're able to accomplish.

Persistence is Important

By now, you can probably guess that persistence is one of the key ingredients in successfully helping your aging parents. You may need several years to convince your parents they need physical and mental checkups. They may resist all your efforts to become involved in their affairs until you mention the idea fifty or a hundred times. You may also need to keep coaxing other family members to visit more often or to share more of the caregiving responsibilities.

The outside world is no easier. Insurance and government bureaucracies are slow to respond, and rarely get things right on the first attempt. If the family decides your parents should move, you'll need extra persistence to make all the needed arrangements, move them out of their present home, find them a new place to live and get them settled in.

Persistence also helps you endure when improvements come very slowly. In many families, adult children don't start taking much responsibility until their parents' problems become very serious. If you wait this long, your first challenges may involve many different problems — with physical, mental, emotional, financial, legal and family overtones — all clamoring for immediate attention. You'll need persistence — and patience — to identify the separate problems, put them in priority order, and take steps to improve them while you try to maintain your own life, work and relationships.

To make sure you have the strength and willpower to persist, attempt no more than you can reasonably manage over a long period of time. Many problems take longer than several months to resolve. You'll provide more help if you do a little at a time, but keep on doing it for the long haul. Keep pushing until you get the best possible services or situation for your aging parents. Don't accept less than a satisfactory outcome, no matter how long it takes. In this way, you'll keep peeling away layers of bureaucratic resistance and sloth. Of course, not all problems can be solved, but while you're making the effort, you'll have the emotional satisfaction of being with your parents and helping them.

CHAPTER 6

FAMILY ISSUES

In many respects, caring for aging parents is like child rearing. Nearly everyone faces very similar demands, problems, and emotional ups and downs. However, no two families ever face exactly the same circumstances in raising young children or caring for aging parents, and no single set of answers or choices can be entirely satisfying to everyone.

That's why this book doesn't try to offer pat answers to even the most common problems. One family's good solution simply won't work as well for another. Instead of providing prepackaged procedures, the goal is to aid you to better understand your family's exact situation and to foster a process that will help your family define its problems and solve them in its own special way.

As discussed in other chapters of this book, you must understand all the medical, financial, emotional, legal and practical issues confronting you and your aging parents. Making decisions about how best to care for your parents is a ticklish process. It's fraught with all sorts of complications, restrictions, personal preferences and idiosyncrasies that can make any choice seem undesirable from at least one point of view. Any decision-making within a family is complicated, and urgent pressure to help your parents only makes it tougher. To ease the family through this trying time, you must understand how your family operates as well as how to help your parents.

Cooperative Family Action

You may have the time, money and emotional resources to do everything for your parents without help from anyone else in the family. More likely, you'll already have a full plate of responsibilities, and you'll have to add your efforts for your parents on top. Your best chance to get your parents all the help they need will be to involve other family members in a coordinated plan of action, and to prevent anyone from working at cross purposes.

You may decide Mom and Dad should take a smaller apartment, give up their car and have at least one meal a day brought in. Unless you get other family members to agree with your ideas and help carry them out, you're probably going to handle all the moving, driving, cooking and other responsibilities on your own.

Should you decide to place your father in a nursing home, you won't want your sister telling him there are better places for him to live. That kind of family conflict will cause your father unnecessary distress. He'll feel better if everyone he loves and trusts agrees on the nursing home, and supports his steady adjustment to it. As in any other endeavor, family members will help your parents best only when they have a strong hand in developing the plan of action.

In general, the family should try to function as a team. One or two people who communicate best with Mom and

Dad should stay in closest contact with them, monitoring their health and well-being, and being the primary ones to discuss with them or advise them of family concerns and recommendations. The other family members can contribute from their own strengths, taking on some of the overall responsibility and doing a fair share of the work.

The Impact of Family History

By the time your parents need help, members of your extended family — including you, your parents, your children, your brothers and sisters, your aunts and uncles, all their children, anyone married to any of these people and all *their* children — have a lot of shared history. That history usually includes both good and bad times, people arguing and airing major differences, fights that produced losers as well as winners, plain old personality conflicts, and dozens of other sources of contention and disaffection. In other words, yours is probably a pretty normal family.

All this family history produces a complex web of interrelationships, preferences and personalities that make a family discussion a fragile experience — even under the best of circumstances. When the family is emotionally upset and under pressure to care for one of its own, a family discussion can be seriously hamstrung. You're much less likely to arrive at a workable agreement that satisfies everyone.

For example, Harry Lankin had deteriorated to the point where living in an apartment of his own presented many obstacles. When Harry crashed the car en route to the grocery store, injuring himself and his wife, Rosemary, it was obvious to their children that some changes had to be made immediately. Duncan, their Rosemary's oldest son, felt most responsible. He had the family over for dinner and consultations he hoped would lead to decision-making. However, old animosities, jealousies and personal feuds flared up at every turn, and they were unable to agree on whether the older pair should move, who should take care of them, who should manage their finances, or even which doctor they should use. After three hours of wrangling, Duncan's uncle Jay left in a huff, his sister Kathy broke down in tears and his other sister Judy accused everyone but herself of total selfishness. The Lankin family had great difficulty making any useful decisions, forcing Harry and Rosemary to suffer for months at home until their adult children could finally agree on arrangements for better care.

Many people naively assume that Mom and Dad's urgent needs will make everyone forget their part in the family's history. All too often, this doesn't happen. In most families, the need to care for aging parents can easily trigger another round of the same old family battles that have been going on for years.

Regardless of how poorly your family works together, however, your parents will still need caregiving. Important decisions often can't wait, so you may have to accept some trade-offs. Someone must take responsibility for providing the direct, hands-on care for your parents, or at least for helping the family reach the best decisions. If that someone is you, you'll find it's a very demanding role to play.

Old patterns of interaction are hard to break. For example, if you're not usually the one who keeps family discussions moving forward, you may find it hard to do so. Those who more frequently take charge of family matters won't want to give up their position, and those who are accustomed to others taking charge won't readily listen to you.

Nonetheless, you want to keep your family focused on the main agenda: what to do about your aging parents. Encourage people to put aside their differences, to ignore old family squabbles, and to settle old scores. When you keep the family focused on your parents' immediate problems, you have a much better chance of finding reasonable solutions.

New Family Business

In addition to opening old wounds and fighting old battles, various family members are likely to develop new rivalries, problems and disagreements that stem directly from your parents' decline and need for help.

Although brothers, sisters, aunts, or uncles can spark most of the family conflict when you start caring for your aging parents, your spouse may also have problems supporting you. Parenting your aging parents can put a severe strain on your marriage — one that some spouses are unable to tolerate.

For everyone in the family, **money** is almost always a big issue, even when no one talks about it directly. Caring for Mom or Dad can be an expensive proposition. Some family members may lobby for certain solutions that minimize the amount they're expected to pay. Others may want to pay extra to feel less guilty or to avoid direct caregiving responsibility. In a few families, caring for Mom or Dad is a profitable occupation. Whoever controls their assets may have far more influence, prestige, wealth and power than before. In cases like this, some may try to win control, while others may try to prevent certain people from taking charge. In complicated situations, some may refuse to support doing the "right thing" for Mom or Dad because it benefits someone else in the family. Naturally, none of this helps your parents.

Power is another potential source of trouble. Talks with many families have underscored the advantages of consulting too many people in the family rather than too few, of being overly concerned with family members' opinions and preferences rather than ignoring them. You want everyone to feel involved in the process of caring for Mom and Dad. However, this approach is difficult to manage. From certain perspectives — perhaps your own — this continuous consultation will be a nuisance, a waste of time, or an insult. Many people prefer to feel they have the clout to decide what's to be done without asking others. In extreme cases, someone may be more concerned with taking charge than with doing the best for your aging parents. He or she may live far away, or may visit every day, may do little to help, or may do the bulk of the work. It doesn't matter; one person trying to overrule or ignore others' preferences is certain to create problems.

Responsibility is usually the biggest bone of contention. You'll probably find most family members are willing to give lip service to accepting responsibility. But when it comes time to drive, cook, clean, or visit, and actually deliver on their promises, they become much less available. Many people try to delay the day when their parents first need help from the family.

On the other hand, some family members may become angry and jealous because they are not asked or allowed to offer real help. In the Kinney family, Heather and her husband Harold went to great lengths to care for her mother, Cynthia, after Heather's dad died suddenly. Heather seriously believed her sisters, Patricia and Laura, were too busy to help their mother and were grateful that she took responsibility. But one night at a family gathering Patricia and Laura showed they were extremely angry with Heather. They accused her of being manipulative and selfish. They complained about Heather steadily turning down their countless offers to help. Heather was completely shocked, but agreed to change. Afterwards her sisters began assuming more of the caregiving responsibilities, allowing Heather and Howard to spend less time with her mother. Within a few weeks they were surprised at how good they felt having more time and energy for themselves and their children.

In some families, it may be necessary to let several people take responsibility for a chore that any one of them could do — not because they're all needed, but because they all want to be involved. This arrangement creates extra coordination problems, though, and can leave a chore undone if each person thinks another is handling it. In other families, some people will be more than happy to let one brother or sister take the bulk of the responsibility for Mom and Dad. Try not to be angered or distracted by any of this family maneuvering. Keep focused on what's really important: doing the best you can for your parents.

Sibling and Family Squabbles

Under pressure of caring for aging parents, family members (particularly brothers and sisters) can magnify conflicts or bad feelings all out of proportion.

In the Benning family, for example, Ronald was proud and happy that he and his wife, Constance, took primary responsibility for Ronald's aging parents, Sidney and Bea. Ronald managed their finances and maintained their home. Constance oversaw and coordinated the contributions of half a dozen community services and organizations, needed to help keep Sidney and Bea healthy and happy. Ronald and Constance held up well under the pressure for the first two years. But one day at a birthday party for Ronald's youngest sister, a major family blow-up occurred. By the time the dust settled, virtually everyone had accused everyone else of harboring an ulterior motive, betraying someone's trust or violating a confidence. These feelings had apparently been festering ever since Sidney and Bea began needing help. Within a month, Ronald became a nervous wreck and Constance started crying regularly. No one else in the family offered to relieve them of their responsibilities, but everyone felt dissatisfied with their decisions on behalf of Mom or Dad.

There's no easy cure for such problems. Ronald and Constance Benning eventually found ways to shift some caregiving responsibilities to his brothers and sisters. They began using a little more of Sidney and Bea's money to have the housekeeper stay longer most days and prepare their parents' evening meal. They consulted with family members more on many decisions. Eventually, the Benning family regained a fairly even emotional keel, but other families experience such conflicts and misunderstandings for many years.

One reason for conflict may be that your spouse objects to the decisions you're making for your parents. He or she may want you to let others take more responsibility, or may argue that your way of handling things does your parents more harm than good. Your spouse can have a private agenda, too, and may recommend decisions that go against your best judgment. Conflict can also arise when the time and energy you devote to your parents directly reduces the attention you give your spouse and children. These conflicts can make life very trying, so it's important to discuss all these issues with your spouse and to agree as much as possible. Be sure you all know what's in store before you accept too much responsibility for your aging parents.

Another source of conflict is the pressure of having to care for aging relatives who are not your parents. There may be many layers of feelings in conflict with each other when your in-laws, step-parents, or others need your help while your natural parents do not. You may have feelings of resentment and anger at this when your own parents are healthy, and feelings of loneliness and depression over caregiving responsibilities when your own parents are deceased — particularly if you did not directly provide care for them.

One of the most complex family situations arises when you don't get along with your parents or the in-laws who need your help. There may be a general personality conflict, or some long-standing, specific and very good reason for the lack of warmth between you. In some cases, you're not able or needed to help your own parents, and you wind up devoting time and energy you can't really spare from your other responsibilities to take care of in-laws or relatives you don't like very much.

An equally complex problem arises when one parent becomes angry at another. In many families, aging parents simply don't get along, and caring for them often places you squarely between the warring parties. Even when parents are still united, however, an able parent is likely to experience some anger, frustration, and resentment toward a disabled one, and to expect you to share these feelings.

The caregiving situation can also become very convoluted when Mom has expectations about her daughter, or when a daughter feels a special obligation toward her parents. Many adults have a hard time feeling fully independent, and having to be responsible for aging parents can create a new basis for family conflicts.

There is no easy way out of these problems. If you're lucky, there will be someone else in the family ready, willing and able to take on a good portion of the caregiving responsibility, in which case you can try to limit yourself to a supporting role. If no one else shoulders enough responsibility, however, you may have to grit your teeth and provide the direct help you feel is needed. As with other complex family situations, try to forthrightly explore your feelings. Express them to others in your life, and try to do what you feel is right for you in the situation.

In most families, the person who takes responsibility for aging parents tends to receive the brunt of family displeasure. Others may be feeling guilty about doing less than you, or jealous of the special closeness they see developing between you and your aging parents. Frequently, family members will express these feelings as criticism of your efforts, particularly if they — like most people — find it easier to fault other's work than to take direct responsibility. You personally may not be the target of anyone's criticism or bad feelings. But if you take on the caregiving responsibility, be ready for a brother or sister to come after you for something you feel you haven't done, or worse, for something you feel you've done very well or at substantial personal sacrifice.

One frequent basis for criticism is your "selfish" behavior, particularly when helping your aging parents helps you at the same time. For example, after Fern (Morgan) rented her parents an apartment in the complex near her house, she began making free use of their fitness center. When Bill Ford was talking with his father-in-law Addison Williams' broker, he heard a few profitable investment ideas for his own funds. After Jan (Hinckley) spent so much time and effort helping her parents move to the elevator apartment, her mother decided to give her the china and silverware. There's no reason for shame about any of this, provided you don't short-change your parents or other family members in order to help yourself.

The best way to keep yourself safe and sane is to stay aware of your motives. Before you accept any responsibility, think long and hard about why you want it. If helping your parents will also bring you some personal advantage — for example, taking control of Dad's financial empire or getting back at your older brother for upstaging you all the time you were growing up — recognize this.

It's equally important to think carefully about how each of the steps you take — and don't take — impacts your aging parents and everyone else in the family. Examine your motivations, concerns, and preferences before and after you take a particular action. If you decide to place your paralyzed mother in a nursing home, for example, be sure you know whether you're primarily trying to get her the best care or most interested in helping Dad go on with his life. If you don't feel Dad should have a hip replacement, be clear about whether you're primarily worried about sparing him the risk of the surgical procedure or concerned with protecting Dad and the family from suffering through a long, slow recovery period.

Once you know and understand your motivations, you are better prepared for anyone in the family who tries to ambush you with accusations or anger. Should anyone attack you, try to stay away from defensive responses. Focus your replies on what you're doing, and why. Offer to share your caregiving responsibilities.

A good way to keep family squabbles in check is to firmly adhere to what you honestly believe your parents want. Although it's not always possible, the harder you try and the closer you come to this standard the less you'll be hurt by family contention. For example, you may *feel* that your father should be in a nursing home, but *know* that he wants to stay in his own bed as long as possible.

Therefore, you may decide to make an extra effort to keep him home. Others in the family may accuse you of conserving Dad's money so there will be more for you to inherit. However, you and other family members involved in your decision-making process will know your true motivation.

Trying to do what your parents want (or would want if they could express themselves) can create difficult personal conflicts. Estelle Granger, like many wives, was unwilling to see her husband, Dan, placed in a nursing home. Many people who are 60, 70, or 80 years old will nearly work themselves to death trying to care for their incapacitated spouses. You may join the growing ranks of those who have learned it is sometimes necessary to send one parent to a nursing home in order to improve the quality of life for the other. However, if you go against Dad's or Mom's wishes on this or any other decision, make certain you're prepared to live with their disapproval. Otherwise, family squabbles can extract a significant toll on your emotional well-being.

Aside from feeling secure about your decisions, try to remain practical. That is, be sure to follow careful procedures that will help protect you and your good name. Relatives have been known to sue one another because they don't like the way Mom or Dad is being treated. Although most of these lawsuits are frivolous, they must be defended by hiring a lawyer and appearing before a judge. To minimize the trauma of any such defense, at a minimum keep accurate records and use separate accounts for your parents' funds.

A good way to keep family relationships from putting additional strain on your emotions is to be as open and honest with everyone in your family as you possibly can. There's little you can to do stop others from trying to manipulate situations by slanting what they say and do.

There are probably enough demands and pressures on you without adding the need for constant "gamesmanship" and participation in family politics. It's emotionally much easier to be as straight as you can with all comers, without becoming defensive about your actions or feelings. As long as your motives are clear, your intentions are honest, and your efforts are open and aboveboard (and backed up with the right supporting paperwork), you present a much smaller, more resistant target for others' manipulations and attacks.

Sharing Wealth and Bric-A-Brac

One pattern you may see in your aging parents is a strong desire to simplify their lives. They'll stay home more, lose contact with some of their friends, abandon hobbies or other activities that require special gear, and start getting rid of what they feel are excess goods. Your parents may want to give away their china, crystal and silverware, old family photos, tools, clothes they no longer wear and much more. They may also want to distribute their money and other assets, sometimes within the family, sometimes not.

Most adult children feel uncomfortable with this. Some fear it's a sign their parents' lives may suddenly end; others feel uncomfortable with the inevitable discussion of who gets what. Some complain they don't like the things their parents want to give them.

You'll do better if you accept this divesting and simplifying process. You probably can't stop it anyway. Letting your parents make their own decisions and run their own lives as much and for as long as possible is best, even when you don't agree with their actions. The process can be a way for your parents to exercise control over what becomes of their possessions, a right which they deserve. In some families, giving away assets makes good sense for financial and tax purposes. Getting rid of their excess baggage can also help your parents become more comfortable in their home and their lifestyle. Of course, if they lose touch with reality and give valuable antiques or necessities to total strangers, you'll want to step in.

Don't feel embarrassed or reluctant to accept a few gifts you want from your parents. If you have a hard time taking anything, whether family heirlooms or cash, reconsider. Why deny your parents the pleasure of giving you gifts? More important, why shouldn't you be as willing to accept gifts from your parents as you are for others to accept them? If you don't want a beautiful, useful, or meaningful gift from your aging parents, try to understand why.

Never let fights over gifts or any division of goods influence decisions concerning your parents. For example, an adult daughter may covet her mother's dining room furniture well before her mother is ready to give it up. In a perfect world, she would wait patiently. But she may encourage her mother to move to a smaller apartment at least partly in hopes the dining room furniture won't fit. Similarly, a son may be interested in receiving his aging father's power tools, though Dad still has the strength and ability to enjoy using them.

Getting Help

A great many adult children have a strong urge to take on all, or at least most of the responsibility of caring for their aging parents. In many families, that's a mistake. Parents often benefit from the warm feelings other family members express by helping them.

In addition, medical, legal, financial and other specialists can do a better job than you with particular aspects of caregiving. It may well be true that no one is more qualified than you to coordinate the overall responsibility of caring for your parents. But it's almost certainly and equally true that no one is less qualified than you at certain specialized tasks, such as diagnosing medical problems, drawing up legal documents, or analyzing investment opportunities.

Receiving help from family members and professionals makes it easier for you to sustain your effort. You'll benefit from having others with whom you can talk and share your feelings, others who will really understand the situation. Few people can continuously carry the entire load of parental caregiving. At the very least, you'll need an occasional respite.

Respite Care

Organized programs for the physically and emotionally disabled and for children frequently recognize the need for respite care, and arrange for paid workers to provide full-time caregivers from twelve to thirty-six hours of relief time each month. You too can benefit from making the same type of respite arrangements with family members or paid workers such as a home health aide or homemaker. This is time for you, or any caregiver, to relax, enjoy hobbies or friends, and just unwind from the pressure. Respite caregivers also help those receiving care, too, bringing a change of pace and a chance to develop new and stimulating relationships. In addition, the respite caregiver may notice early signs of problems or symptoms that have escaped your attention: a change in your parent's behavior or health status, or subtle signs of too much stress on *you*.

But respite care for an afternoon, a day, or a weekend won't satisfy you if you bring in someone at the last minute. It's far better to rely on someone regularly involved with your parents. That's one good reason to have several family members help care for your parents: it's more likely one of them can take on your responsibilities when you need time off.

Support Groups

A trend among adult children caring for aging parents is to join some kind of support group. These support groups can be general, or can be organized around a specific issue, like Alzheimer's Disease. Group members meet once or twice a week and talk about practical as well as emotional issues in caring for aging parents. Sharing thoughts and feelings with others who face the same problems helps group members cope with the frustration, disappointment, fear, repetition and many thankless tasks that mark the days and nights of caring for aging parents.

The same social service agencies and facilities that offer assistance to your parents will often sponsor this type of support group. For example, a nursing home may organize an Alzheimer's Caregivers' Support Group. A senior adult day center may host a weekly support group for adult caregivers. Community Centers, religious organizations, and groups set up to serve the aged may provide space for or run their own caregiver support groups.

Whether or not the group has a formal leader, the basic format is remarkably similar: Everything said within the group is strictly confidential. Group members are encouraged to explore and reveal their feelings without fear of criticism or rejection. The main agenda, aside from disseminating important factual information, is to provide support for the caregivers' emotions and practical problems. Group members frequently encourage each other to take time off from their caregiving responsibilities.

Although a support group relies on volunteer participation, some organizations that sponsor these groups actually require caregivers to attend. This is because many adult children don't realize they need support and never ask for help. They may find group situations unfamiliar and uncomfortable. By forcing family members to participate in a support group, the organization exposes them to its positive benefits and helps them do their parents more good over a longer period. Experience shows that virtually everyone who participates in a support group gains some benefit.

Senior Adult Day Centers

Whether your parent is living in their own home or with you, one important way to gain some respite from your responsibilities is to enroll them in a senior adult day center.

Like a day care center for pre-schoolers, the senior adult day center is often located in a storefront, community center, or hospital. The one you choose should be an attractive, safe environment staffed by caring people with some special skill, talent and training who enjoy their work.

The programs, activities and people at the senior adult day center can make a significant difference in your parents' lives. Even if only one attends, the other one can gain some free time to rest and enjoy life. At the center, your parents can make new friends, engage in social activities, gain new experiences and find new sources of pleasure. Activities can range from playing cards and bingo to light exercise and knitting. Some centers have occasional live entertainment and most provide TV and films on tape. Some day centers can accommodate a few people confined to wheelchairs or needing help using the bathroom, but those needing heavier care may be unable to attend.

Equally important is the time the day center gives you away from your aging parents. For many devoted caregivers, a few hours of free time can bring a big lift. For those who work, knowing their parent is safe allows them to concentrate more fully on their other responsibilities. As with nursing homes, the senior adult day center frequently benefits the caregivers as much as the aging parents.

A few corporations and other employers, already under pressure to provide child-care assistance, are making strides toward day centers that serve both children and seniors. Although mixing adults who may be cranky, cantankerous, or abusive in their language with young children creates some problems, it leads to wonderful moments and feelings, too. Children spontaneously climb into the lap of an older person to tell a story. Other times, children and their elders collaborate in baking cookies or producing a show.

(At present, senior adult day centers for parents are not easy to find. The best ones usually have long waiting lists. Most have limited hours, no transportation and restrictions for physical handicaps. Costs can be too high for your family. But this probably won't last. Senior adult day centers are certain to become more available and affordable as more families find need of them.)

Caring for the Caregiver

Although your aging parents are typically at much greater risk for illness and death than you are, you aren't invulnerable. Caring for aging parents can significantly drain your emotional and physical strength, and leave you susceptible to sickness or depression. You jeopardize your parents' health and well-being when you neglect your own.

Here are some ideas on how to remain healthy enough to take care of your parents over the long haul:

Keep looking for aspects of your caregiving relationship you enjoy and appreciate. Try to get the most satisfaction you can from the time you spend with your parents or thinking about them. The more fulfillment you can take from the experience, the longer you will be able to avoid emotional burnout.

Keep looking for experiences you enjoy and appreciate outside of your caregiving relationship. Don't become so completely centered on helping that you neglect your own life. You'll be more help to your parents when you have as full and happy a life as possible.

Treat your parents' problems as many different and separate issues. If you view all your parents' difficulties, weaknesses and problems as a single situation, you'll despair of ever improving it. However, if you sort their problems and difficulties into separate elements, you can put them in priority order and tackle them individually. You'll find solutions and remedies more easily attainable. Most important, you'll see more progress and renew your spirit to persist.

Preserve your own health and happiness, and that of your family. Get enough food and sleep. When you feel run-down, get enough rest to restore your strength. Carefully reduce your stress level, under a doctor's supervision, if necessary. Try to rid yourself of stress with a fast round of racquetball or a walk around the park rather than by drinking or smoking. You may want to experiment with meditation or self-realization techniques, which work for many people under stress. If you and your spouse can maintain a united front against pressures from your parents, from your own growing children, and from other family members, you'll find it much easier to endure the daily stress.

Educate yourself about your parents' problems. Read about the physical and emotional conditions they exhibit. Talk with specialists to discover how their medical conditions may change, and how well each type of treatment can work. Go to educational seminars and learn what you can. Your new knowledge will help balance your constantly changing emotions over your parents suffering and your efforts to help them.

Don't work alone, or approach the end of your rope. Seek and accept help from anyone who sincerely offers it. Even if other people have time only for a simple, specific chore, you and your parents can benefit from their contribution. Share your concerns, choices and emotions with friends, family, or professionals who are involved. Attend group activities that can help sustain you. Be sure to do this long before you run out of ideas, options, or the strength to carry on.

Maintain realistic expectations. You can't solve all your parents' problems, restore them to perfect health, or make them young again. The best you can do is try to make their lives more comfortable, improve their quality of life and see them through whatever lies ahead. Expecting anything more is setting yourself up for disappointment and failure.

Allow yourself some negative feelings. Resentment, anger, disappointment and sadness are normal. It's a mistake to punish yourself for these feelings. Try to accept them as a natural response to your situation.

Plan for the long term. If you start helping your parents only after the problems have piled up, the situation may get worse before it gets better. Most people find it easier to develop a day-to-day mentality, trying as hard as they can to cope with immediate problems and allowing no thought for tomorrow. Focusing on today's troubles is generally a good strategy. It's also necessary, however, to develop a flexible, far-sighted plan that helps you obtain long-term solutions to your parents' problems.

Making Decisions

It's neither fair nor appropriate for the family to make decisions that influence your parents without consulting them and considering their own stated preferences and desires. Most of these family decisions at one time belonged exclusively to Mom and Dad. If your parents are to remain as independent as possible for as long as possible, you must include them in making all the relevant decisions.

Try to find out what your parents really want before decisions are actually made. Parental wishes should go into your parent's wills and other legal documents, but the family can also openly discuss them. The happiest families tend to be those in which the adult children have done their homework well before their parents' incapacities drop important decisions into the family's collective lap. It seems that if the family has a good idea about what Mom or Dad would want, people find it easier to put that idea into practice.

Of course, it may be impractical for your parents to attend the family gathering directly. They may be confined to a hospital bed, or be too weak or ill. They may not understand the discussion or the options available to them. Or you may decide exposing them to a strained and argumentative family discussion would be too stressful.

Nevertheless, you can talk over the situation with your parents and get a feeling for their preferences. Or the family can select two or three options that you can calmly and patiently present to your parents and ask for their thoughts and feelings. You may feel it's enough just to tell them what the family is considering, and later the decisions. However you do it, keep your parents involved in the decision-making process as much as possible.

Though it's difficult, try your best to distinguish between decisions that are primarily good for you or for the family and those primarily good for your aging parents. Put your energy toward keeping your parents' wishes and needs in the forefront of family decision-making.

Every family has its own special interpersonal dynamics, so it's impossible to give you specific instructions on how your family should actually make its decisions. However, caring for aging parents does seem to work out better when key family members make decisions together. These are the people with the strongest emotional ties to your parents, those most affected by the problem and the solution, and those who must put the decision into action.

For example, don't simply inform a nephew who loves your Mom that you're planning to confine her to a nursing home; get him involved. Perhaps he can provide a better alternative than anyone else in the family. Similarly, don't force a younger sister still in college to find part-time work because the family can't afford both her college education and a new, better situated home for your parents. Don't assume she can't or won't voluntarily contribute to the solution. Instead, get her ideas and understanding before you take any actions.

Most important, don't allow anyone to simply assign family members their chores and responsibilities. If the caregiving plan relies on a daughter's willingness to cook for Mom and Dad three times a week, make sure she has participated in developing that plan. Otherwise, she may be unable to live up to the commitment over the long haul, and she will certainly be angry and resentful.

However, there may be times when you must make decisions on your own, particularly in emergencies: Should Dad be placed on a respirator? Will Mom be fed through tubes? Aside from emergencies, many other decisions don't need the entire family's consideration: Should your parents take a first floor or second floor apartment? At which bank should they open checking and savings accounts? Are they well enough to fly 500 miles to attend a wedding? Countless decisions have some, but no major impact on your parents' health or quality of life. These are times you may want to choose a course of action by yourself, or with just one or two advisors.

CHAPTER 7

DEATH-RELATED ISSUES

The end of all caregiving is death. It's an unpleasant subject, rarely comfortable for family members to discuss or endure. Yet no book on parenting your aging parents would be complete without some discussion of the inevitable.

Emotional Issues

One of the most difficult subjects to talk about, or prepare for, is the death of a parent. It involves a wide range of emotions, and requires you to deal with anxiety and to consider your own death. Death can come quickly to an aging parent, but most times there is some warning. While never pleasant, heeding this warning can help the family suffer less emotional trauma than might otherwise occur. Since you can't avoid death, you should try to prepare for it.

Preparing for the Inevitable

As you help your parents maintain the best possible quality of life, you may encounter more and more reminders that death is coming closer. Your parents may show signs of physical weakness and decline, and lose some ability to concentrate or converse. They may suffer more frequent illnesses and accidents.

Contemplating your parent's death can be doubly unpleasant. In addition to the sadness of Mom or Dad's demise, the event can force you to consider your own mortality, and confront the fear and anxiety that come with such thoughts. Exploring your thoughts and feelings, and talking about death-related issues well in advance of any need are good ways to prepare for (and possibly to reduce your anxiety in the face of) your parent's impending death.

It's best to be open and honest with your parents about death. They have the right to know the truth about their physical condition and their prospects for the future. Most adult children expect their parents to break down on news of impending death. But a surprising number can accept the news fairly well.

Some adult children have more trouble preparing for death than their aging parents. If Mom tries to begin sentences with: "When I'm gone...," a loving daughter or son might immediately interrupt and urge: "Don't say that. You'll live forever." But this may do more harm than good. When caregivers let their own fear dominate, they can make a person less comfortable talking about death, and thus interfere with his or her ability to prepare for it. Adult children who are comfortable with their feelings about death seem far better able to help their parents during this difficult time.

A fruitful approach is to talk about concrete issues of real concern and importance: the details of funeral arrangements, disposition of property, shuffling of family responsibilities, and so forth. By concentrating on these points, many families first broach the subject of death. Naturally, you won't want to pressure your parents to dwell on death more than they are willing. But with tender consideration over a period of days, weeks, or months, you may help your parents come closer to accepting their own or a loved one's approaching death.

When death occurs, you're forced into mourning. No matter how much or how well you have prepared for it, the death of your parent is never easy. For Mom or Dad, the death of their life partner is especially painful, even if it comes after many years of slow deterioration. Every action, every feeling, every sight and sound can vividly remind them of the person no longer alive to share it.

It's important to establish some basis for living after the death of a loved one. Most people appear to suffer less and go on with their lives more easily if they have maintained an active lifestyle and cultivated strong relationships within and without the family. For adult children, there is almost always a solid basis for a full life away from Mom or Dad. For an aging couple, however, the surviving spouse may need to form new relationships and seek out new activities to replace the time and energy once spent with the deceased.

It's a frequent pattern among older couples for one partner to become ill and the other to devote him- or herself to caregiving. This can work well for quite a while. Yet when death ultimately takes one spouse — usually the weaker one, but not always — the survivor has nothing as important with which to replace that relationship. The result can be a severe depression or illness, and a period of adjustment through which the entire family can suffer.

If you're not unduly shy about preparing for your parent's eventual death, your family may be able to circumvent some or all of this pattern. Start today, even if you are convinced your parents will live for many more years. Encourage them to lead active lives, to maintain old friendships and develop new ones, and to keep up with hobbies or interests. It's particularly beneficial when Mom and Dad each have at least a few of their own friends and their own favorite activities. When death takes one partner from this type of lifestyle, the survivor feels much more continuity, less devastation, and more chance for continued happiness because of the remaining ties to people and interests.

Statistically, a woman is likely to live about seven years longer than her mate. You can see the proof everywhere you go, particularly in retirement communities and other places where elderly people congregate. About **twenty percent of men** over 65 are widowers, but more than **fifty percent of women** over 65 are widows. The chance of outliving a husband is so high that most women should prepare — or be prepared by their adult children — to become widows. This means Mom should know where to find important documents, acquire some basic knowledge of the family's financial affairs, and get to know the family accountant, lawyer and other advisors familiar with the details.

Accepting One's Own Death

No matter how much illness or suffering parents experience, they may not know death is close by. Even if they feel desperately ill, they still may not openly admit or discuss the possibility of death. Most aging parents who feel life slipping away hope for a quick and painless end, but in many families death comes slowly. A depressing incapacity can last for years. There may be physical deterioration and pain. There may also be some form of mental deterioration, which can rob your parent of the ability to understand or choose alternatives, to sign needed papers, or to consider and prepare for death.

It isn't easy to find words or useful activities to help your aging parents adjust to the inevitable. Nevertheless, you must try. In general, people will retain their hope to their last breath, waiting for a miracle cure or a remission. Don't try to take this hope away. Optimism strengthens the will to live, and may help keep your Mom or Dad alive a little longer.

As your parent faces death, he or she may go through a personal grief period, progressing through strong emotional stages that start with denial and end with acceptance. Dr. Elisabeth Kubler-Ross has written extensively on this emotional progression in her landmark book: *On Death And Dying*.

Essentially, Dr. Kubler-Ross and other researchers have identified five emotional stages that dying people will often pass through, provided they have enough time. These stages include the denial of death, anger at the finality of death, bargaining to avoid death, depression and acceptance.

Denial: During the denial stage, your parent is likely to refuse to believe that death is so entirely certain. He or she may feel a doctor or lab technician has made a mistake, or may refuse to accept the validity of a test or a diagnosis. This open denial can serve a valuable purpose, giving your parent more time to become accustomed to impending death, and to begin tying up loose ends and relationships.

Responding to a parent who is going through denial is tricky. On one hand, it's useless and cruel to browbeat them with the reality of their impending death. On the other hand, it's pointless to pretend that death is not approaching. In most cases, it's best to follow a middle course: Allow Mom or Dad to persist in denying death, while you continue to prepare as much as possible. Your behavior indicating the certainty of death can help your parent work through the denial stage.

Anger: The anger that follows denial can also create family problems. Your parent may become angry at you, your children, medical attendants, anyone or anything. The anger usually comes in waves they cannot control. When the wave passes, it may be replaced by guilt. When Mom or Dad becomes irascible, understand this anger as a sign your parent is making progress toward accepting the certainty of death.

Bargaining: The usual bargaining pattern has the dying person withdrawing from normal contact with family members and privately negotiating with God or some higher power. Internally, Mom or Dad will promise a change of behavior or repentance for past mistakes in return for more time to live. In many families, a parent will bargain to live just long enough to see an important event, such as the birth of a baby, or a birthday, wedding, or anniversary. There may be something to this bargaining. Curiously, researchers have found a significant number of older people die just *after* important milestones like their birthday or a major holiday.

Depression: The onset of depression shows your parent has begun to realize no amount of anger or negotiation can postpone death. Mom or Dad now begins to feel very deeply the loss of good health, of enjoyable activities, and the impending separation from loved ones. Your parent may also feel more of a burden to others in the family, or regret over having caused sadness and pain. Some parents become depressed over knowing they will never experience events far in the future, like a young grandchild's college graduation or wedding. This depression stage can prove very trying, painful, and sad for the rest of the family, but provides a positive sign that your parent is closer to accepting his or her own death.

Acceptance: The acceptance stage is the culmination of this emotional roller coaster. Although often tired and weak, people in this stage are generally calm and peaceful. Their emotions tend to be steadier than usual. They may retreat into themselves, wanting fewer visitors and shorter visits. Acceptance is the most positive emotion a dying person can experience. It leads to a serenity in which your parent can enjoy both current experiences and distant memories, and can view death as a welcome release rather than a dreaded enemy.

Unfortunately, many people never reach acceptance of their own death. Some die before they make the full adjustment. Others don't progress past an earlier emotional stage (perhaps because their family cannot accept the situation and help them adjust to it). Some move to a later stage, but then fall back. A few, particularly those who are not told the truth about their illness or injuries, may continue in denial. However, experience indicates that most dying people who have enough time, and who are properly encouraged, can eventually accept their impending death.

As a parent nears death, the spouse and children may echo some or all of these emotional stages. There is little you can do to defuse the anger or short-circuit the depression and other unpleasant emotions associated with a loved one's approaching death. But family members who understand this process can support each other and make the process of death more endurable.

Feeling Grief

Psychiatrists and psychologists have discovered grief to be one of the most important features of death. A very complex process, grief encompasses a broad range of emotions — including shock, disorientation, anger, guilt, loneliness, relief and acceptance — that follow any major loss. These feelings are particularly strong after the death of a loved one. However, grief is a healthy response that provides emotional "healing" and allows the grieving person to regain a good deal of their former happiness.

Not everyone exhibits all the emotions of grief, or feels them in the same sequence. One emotion may have much more impact on some individuals than on others. Some people may constantly find their eyes filled with tears at certain sights, sounds, or memories; others may grieve so privately that no one suspects the depth of their sorrow. Whatever the case, you can reduce the trauma of death simply by understanding and anticipating the various stages of grief.

Shock or Denial: Initially, you may not believe your parent is dead. You expect to see them alive again. You wonder why they had to die, and particularly why now. You may think their death was unfair. Younger children may not understand that Grandpa or Grandma will never come back.

Disorientation: This is a period of confusion, disinterest in normal routines, and forgetfulness about details such as where you left the car keys, which clothes to wear and what foods to eat. Some family members may cry or stare sadly into space. Others may ignore responsibilities, make poor decisions, suffer sleep disturbances, or withdraw completely from normal life. Encourage everyone to behave as they feel, and not to be too hard on themselves or others for shortcomings or emotional reactions. Bottled up emotions can lead to deeper problems later on.

Anger: People in the family will begin to express anger or resentment at any convenient target, including the deceased. It's normal to wonder "How could she do this to me?" or to think "This was the worst possible time for this to happen," or "Why couldn't I have made him take better care of himself?" Younger children may feel betrayed by parents who failed to "warn" them in strong enough terms that Grandma or Grandpa would die when they did.

Guilt: People will also begin to regret that they cannot complete all the unfinished business in their relationships with the deceased, or take back any thoughtless remarks. Some may say: "I wish I had been at his side when he died," or: "If only I had been nicer to her." These thoughts generally represent strong emotions that people should be free to express without contradiction or debate.

Loneliness: Most family members will experience a sense of profound loneliness, frequently expressed as sadness, depression, self-pity, or another emotion. These feelings may last a long time unless you make strong efforts to continue with the business of living.

Relief: Though few people want to talk about it, relief is the "hidden" emotion in grief. You may feel free of a burden or of limits. It's important not to feel guilty about relief, and to openly express what you feel rather than pretend.

Acceptance: It may take time, but virtually everyone comes to accept the death of a loved one. Although you shouldn't rush through the other emotions, neither should you resist coming to this stage. Acceptance of a death is natural and healthy.

As you might expect, each of these emotions fights for supremacy within the grieving individual, and you may not always be able to identify which is dominant at a given moment. You needn't worry. Simply understanding the components of grief and allowing yourself to feel them without undue constraints will help you ease the pain of your loss.

While burying a parent reflects the natural order of the generations, and is usually much less traumatic than burying a spouse, a brother or sister, or a child, the death of a parent is never comfortable. Symbolically, it makes you an "orphan." Mature adults will burst into tears long after their parent's death, reminded of their dead mother or father for no apparent reason. Even people 50 or 60 years of age report deep feelings of loss and loneliness after a parent's death.

Neither psychologists nor psychiatrists have established any guidelines on the appropriate amount of time for grief. In addition to ordinary feelings of grief, the death of your parent can have a special impact for certain people. It's best to allow each person to grieve in their own way and time: if the cycle is artificially disturbed — by family pressure, for instance — the sense of loss can persist far longer.

Easing the Emotional Penalty

A parent's death is never easy, but you may suffer less if you are lucky enough to spend time with Mom or Dad during the last days and weeks. If he or she can converse, these visits create good opportunities to reminisce about your lives together, but the real benefit is the emotions and thoughts you share that will help you later on.

Although it's a very trying time, do your best to keep the relationship between you and your parent clean and simple. Trivial disagreements a few hours or days before your parent's death can haunt you for years afterwards. Obviously, you and your parent may have your differences, but as Mom or Dad weakens and comes closer to death, try to end every conversation with a warm and positive feeling.

When your parent is gone, you'll have to carry on as best you can. Years ago, when people lived in villages and small communities, they received plenty of support for open grieving and public displays of their emotion. Today, you may not know most of your neighbors, who can easily leave you alone in private grief. This is one reason why your immediate family becomes such an important source of emotional support after the death of your parent.

Of course, family members are all unique individuals. Some relatives are uncomfortable talking about death, or expressing their grief. Others may feel embarrassed, and may want to find a private place for grieving away from the rest of the family. A parent's death can bring a close family closer, but it can also can split family members apart. Much depends on the family's relationships before the death occurred. In any case, this is a traumatic event that can disrupt a family for several years.

A parent's death can create emotional problems when you don't give yourself the time to experience all your emotions. Many adult children return to work and other responsibilities within a few days. When an older parent dies, people tend to have less sympathy and tolerance for the intensity of the emotions you may feel. Although you want to help others in your family, it's best to take care of your own emotions first. In many families, one person seems the strongest, comforting and helping everyone else through their grief. But he or she may be doing this partly to avoid facing a whirlwind of frightening feelings. For many years to come, this "pillar of strength" may have the worst problems adjusting to a parent's death. Only after you accept your own feelings about the death of your

Mom or Dad can you concentrate on providing comfort and support to others.

Practical Issues

The process of parenting your aging parents gives rise to many financial, legal and practical problems — and some of the most important are related to death. In most cases, it's wise to determine all the facts of the matter and to think carefully about a situation before committing to a course of action.

But it's wrong to spend so much time studying a problem that you delay too long in making decisions. You can modify or reverse many choices at a later date, so you and your parents don't have to get everything exactly right the first time around. The most important thing is to start early enough.

As a rule, you and your parents should consider their legal and financial options and problems at least once a year. Take these opportunities to refine earlier strategies and decisions. Very often, you'll find people have had changes of heart, or conditions have changed. Some decisions that once looked good will now look much less attractive. Take steps to improve whatever you can.

Legal and Financial Matters

Even before your parents begin to weaken, it is important to execute legal documents that specify who can act for them, when, and in what capacities. Because all these legal arrangements generally happen "within the family," many people want to handle them with verbal agreements or unspoken "understandings." This is dangerous. During the months and years ahead there will be too many opportunities for misunderstandings, for changes of heart, and for emotion-laden battles in which reason and logic go out the window. The saner, safer approach is to put every agreement, understanding and financial responsibility in writing, and to get all the appropriate signatures.

Most states have complex laws that require a specialist to interpret and to draft the appropriate legal documents. Laws vary from state to state, so your parents should consult a lawyer before finalizing any arrangements. It's better if your parents work with a specialist who is knowledgeable about matters of "elder law" or "family law," and who shares most of their values and supports their preferences. Local bar associations and clergy can refer your parents to several qualified professionals, and they can select the one they feel is best.

When you help them hire a lawyer, it's important to decide "Who is the client?" It may be you, your parents, a group within the family, or the entire family. Because the legitimate interests of adult children may diverge from the interests of aging parents, a good lawyer will want to represent only one side in providing advice and preparing documents.

Three important legal documents your parents can execute include:

A Will. This is the basic legal document by which each individual controls the disposition of his or her estate. Unfortunately, nearly half of all Americans die without a will, and the result is a long and expensive legal headache for survivors. There's no reason to put the family through this. A clear, concise will is simple to prepare. Many states publish sample wills your parents can easily fill in. Lawyers can also draw up simple wills for a relatively low fee.

Your parents should update their wills after every major change in tax laws, and after major personal changes — such as a move to a different state or the sale of the family home. Each parent should leave copies of his or her most recent will with their lawyer, with family members, and possibly in a safe deposit box, so the latest will is always readily available.

A Living Will. In some states, a "living will" is a specialized document in which your parents tell medical professionals exactly what to do *and what not to do* if they become incapacitated or mentally incompetent. Unless your parents sign a document like this, they have no guarantee anyone will be aware of their wishes in these circumstances. These documents are becoming more popular as federal regulations require that health care providers tell people about them and their advantages. However, a living will merely *informs* a doctor and other medical staff about these wishes. It does not *force* anyone to follow them. For this, your parents need a power of attorney.

Durable Power of Attorney. In Chapter Three (Finances), we briefly discuss using a durable power of attorney to help you assume control of your parents' finances. This document is much stronger than a living will; it gives you, or anyone your parents designate, full legal power to act on their behalf for as long as they live. Specifically, you can make decisions regarding medical care that supersede the opinions and preferences of attending physicians, even transferring your parents away from a facility that refuses to honor their wishes.

The word "durable" is critical. In most states, a power of attorney automatically becomes invalid after a court declares a person mentally incompetent. But specific wording will keep a power of attorney valid — or "durable" — in such circumstances. If your parents sign this document purposely to cover the chance they may become incapacitated, it's obviously vital to include the required wording.

In some states, special wording can be added to make the durable power of attorney effective *only* when your parents become mentally incapacitated. While this can protect them in some circumstances, if you have difficulty proving such incapacity when your parents really need help, this power of attorney will do them little good.

Health Care Power of Attorney: Another special case occurs in states which require special wording for a power of attorney to be valid for matters of health care, and particularly for life-and-death decisions. If this applies where your parents may be treated, be sure they include the special wording for a *health care power of attorney* in any such document they execute. Many hospitals are now required by law to ask for one when appropriate.

Living Trust. This is a means of transferring ownership of valuable assets from a person to a separate legal entity: the trust. When your parents die, or become incompetent and can no longer make decisions, control of the trust's assets will shift smoothly to another trustee they have named. This eliminates much of the expense, complexity and inconvenience of handling a conventional estate. It's called a *living trust* because your parents can set one up and, unlike ordinary trusts, control it for *their own benefit*.

To make things more convenient, your parents can make the trust "revocable," retaining the right to make changes in how the trust is organized. Because "revocable" trusts remain essentially under the grantor's control, the government allows them significantly *fewer* tax deduction and deferral benefits than "*irrevocable*" trusts.

Some financial concerns become extremely important only after the death of a parent. If Dad is the one who manages the money and he suddenly dies, Mom may not know how to locate the financial records, pay the bills, or even balance the checkbook.

Spouses should show each other where they keep important documents and records, and brief one another on the details of insurance, mortgages, assets, debts and any contracts they have signed. It also makes sense to have another informed person ready to "back-up" one or both of your parents. This provides for continuity of control so the emotional trauma of a death in the family is not compounded by unanticipated financial and legal demands.

Death Benefits: Life insurance questions — whether to have it; how much to have; what type to purchase, and so forth — are best addressed while your parents are relatively young. After the death of a parent, one practical consideration for surviving family members is how to claim the death benefit to which they are entitled.

Most life insurance companies require a certified copy of the death certificate, and many ask to see the original copy of the policy. Although your parents may have lost track of the policy's whereabouts, insurance policies leave traces you can follow to obtain the necessary documents.

You can discover any term life insurance policies that exist through invoices and the associated cancelled checks, or through possible arrangements with your parents' bank for automatic premium withdrawals. You can uncover cash value policies through correspondence and annual statements from the insurance company. Make inquiries and obtain copies of policies now so the family won't face extra difficulties and delays when you finally make a claim.

Although life insurance companies talk about making death benefits available "immediately" to help a surviving spouse cope with the funeral and other expenses, in reality your family may wait several months before the company actually pays any death benefit. Because hundreds of complications can delay the check, it's wise not to count on receiving any "immediate" money from your parent's life insurance policies.

Funeral Arrangements

Many families have their funeral arrangements made and paid for in advance. If your parents have done this, make sure you know their arrangements and preferences.

Even when you think everything is arranged, a sudden death can place you in the position of grieving for your parent while trying to make decisions about permanent and expensive matters. Elaborate caskets can cost as much as a small car, and desirable cemetery plots can run as much as a casket. Because funeral homes and cemeteries are run to make profits for their owners, there's virtually no ceiling on how much you can spend. A funeral is typically a family's third largest expenditure (after a home and a car). But funerals can be arranged at reasonable prices, particularly if you make the choices before the time of death.

Most funeral homes will help you or your parents pre-plan a funeral. Most will encourage you to pre-pay for the funeral, too. Although funeral prices may be lower today than after several more years of inflation, be careful. The money may do your parents more good earning interest in the bank. Your parents may also move to another city before they die, or the funeral home may go out of business.

Bear in mind that your parents need not be buried in the ground. Many people prefer above-ground burial, while others want to be cremated or buried at sea (a service now offered in some coastal states like California).

Don't guess. You may have to gently broach the subject, but ask your parents. Many parents are perfectly comfortable making these decisions or telling you what they prefer. It's easier if the family has anticipated these matters so the time immediately following a parent's death does not become an exercise in consumerism.

Coping With Daily Chores

Among many older couples, there's a strict division of labor. This can create problems when one partner dies and the other must learn to prepare meals, launder clothes, replace fuses, deal with a bank or insurance company, and otherwise handle the mundane chores required for modern living.

One way to help your surviving parent is to fill in for the deceased. While it can be helpful to do all the chores that someone else usually did for Mom or Dad, you may want to go further and help your parent become more self-sufficient. For example, Manuel Gonzalez helped his mother learn to manage her cash and other assets, something she never had to do while his father, Emilio, was alive. While your surviving parent may not enjoy these responsibilities, and may never be good at them, Mom or Dad may still benefit from learning how to take care of themselves, from mastering a new skill, and from appreciation of their increased independence.

"Right To Die" Issues

As medical science continues to develop more effective ways to treat illness and to prolong life, one day you and your parents may have to strike a balance between *life* and *quality of life*, and determine whether an unsatisfactory quality of life is worth maintaining. There are particular considerations regarding how much medical care to provide, and under what conditions to use "heroic measures" to extend your parent's life. Some family members have no doubt that prolonging human life at any cost is always the right course of action. Others are uncertain about the value of using vigorous artificial measures to sustain people who have little contact with reality. Few people faced these questions until recently, when medical science began forcing the dilemma upon us.

A large and growing majority of Americans say they would want their doctors to stop all life-sustaining efforts if they were unavoidably dying and in pain, or if they should become totally incapable of caring for and feeding themselves. An overwhelming majority also favor "right-to-die" laws that allow terminally ill patients to choose death over life. Most states now reflect this sentiment with some type of legislation, and hospital authorities are working on policies and guidelines under which family and physicians may withhold or withdraw life-sustaining efforts.

However, most people recognize a difference between deciding to end *one's own life* in the face of pain and terminal illness, and making the decision for someone else. Although many people understand that certain actions by others seem justified, relatively few are willing to take an active part in ending a loved one's life, even if pain and death seem unavoidable.

Many factors can influence how a person feels about the issue of voluntarily ending the life of a terminally ill person: religious doctrine and beliefs, other values and ethics, previous exposure to death and dying, and specific knowledge of medical treatments and their effects. One of the most influential factors can be how close to home this issue strikes. When people are young and vigorous, they usually consider death to be abstract and remote —

the very last thing they want. However, with advancing age, terminal illness and pain, they may begin to see death as a welcome release from steady suffering and increasing indignities.

A "right to die" generally makes the most sense to family members when aging parents no longer recognize anyone or their surroundings, cannot care for themselves and require extraordinary measures merely to stay alive, or when they suffer constant pain, live under heavy medications and are unable to experience anything of the life and the family they once knew. There are also cases in which the cost of maintaining a suffering parent's life exhausts the family's financial resources and condemns the aging parent's loved ones to years of financial strain and penury.

Some people suffering multiple illnesses and disabilities with little or no "quality of life" are quietly allowed to pass on. In the Kim family, Gloria developed a trusting relationship with the staff and administrator of the nursing home where Dean, her husband, was ultimately confined after major physical and mental deterioration left him totally bedridden, completely disoriented, and unable to eat. As it became apparent Dean was in the advanced stages of Alzheimer's, the administrator helped Gloria write a letter requesting that, although he should be kept as comfortable as possible, no "heroic measures" should be taken to keep Dean alive. Within six months of reaching this totally uncommunicative and deteriorated condition, he died of a massive systemic infection. Without the agreement to avoid "heroic measures," doctors might have moved Dean to a hospital for immediate, aggressive medical treatment. He might have lingered for additional weeks or months, dependent on elaborate machinery, disrupting the lives of the Kim family members and costing them tens of thousands of dollars. The family unanimously agreed that Dean Kim, had he been able to choose, would have preferred the relatively quick death he experienced to an extended and expensive period of medical intervention.

Most families, however, cannot count on such cooperation from doctors, nurses, social workers and other professionals who face a quagmire of professional, legal and practical concerns, as well as their own personal beliefs. Most health care professionals find it extremely onerous to allow a patient to die. Hospitals, in particular, are strongly oriented toward sustaining any vestige of life at any cost. Your parents — and others in your family — may therefore want to consider these issues in some depth and, before the situation arises, take appropriate steps to help assure their wishes will be carried out.

There are no easy solutions. But it's important to consider the options and possibilities. Family members should talk about their feelings, beliefs, objections, and preferences in great detail. Everyone involved should try to participate in the decision-making process, and should make an honest effort to feel comfortable with the family's decisions. Once these issues are decided, each of your parents should record their wishes where they will have the strongest impact: in the appropriate legal documents. If one of your parents is too incapacitated to decide, the family should try to develop consensus decisions regarding what they believe Mom or Dad would want. However, at such a late date it may require establishing full legal guardianship to guarantee that your parent will be treated as he or she would wish.

RESOURCE GUIDE

Checklist for Immediate Action:

1. Check your aging parents' present living situation for health, safety, and convenience. Make any necessary adjustments or begin considering possible adjustments if and when necessary.

2. Obtain a signed *durable power of attorney* from each of your aging parents, preferably with all applicable *health care power of attorney* provisions included.

3. Obtain a signed *living will* or other document from each of your aging parents that sets forth his or her wishes for life support and other medical treatment, for use should they become incompetent to give direction on their own.

4. Make a plan and obtain the necessary signed legal documents for managing your aging parents' assets should they become incapacitated.

5. Check your parents' life and health insurance policies, and help them make any needed adjustments.

6. Do the same for yourself and your spouse.

Federal Government Agencies:

National Institute on Aging
Federal Building, Room 6C12
Bethesda, MD 20892
301-496-1752

Social Security Administration
U.S. Department of Health and Human Services
Bethesda, MD 21235
800-234-5772
(or consult your local office)

Health Care Financing Administration
U.S. Department of Health and Human Services
6325 Security Boulevard
Baltimore, MD 21207
(for Medicare information)

U.S. Department of Labor
Pension and Welfare Benefit Program
200 Constitution Avenue, NW
Washington, DC 20216

U.S. Dept of Health and Human Services
Information on hospital care for indigent
800-638-0742

State Agencies on Aging

Alabama Commission on Aging
502 Washington Avenue
Montgomery, AL 36130
205-261-5743

Alaska Older Citizens Commission
Department of Administration
Pouch C — Mail Station 0209
Juneau, AK 99811
907-465-3250

American Samoa Territorial Administration on Aging
Office of the Governor
Pago Pago, American Samoa 96799
011-684-633-1252

Arizona Aging and Adult Administration
Department of Economic Security
1400 West Washington Street
Phoenix, AZ 85007
602-255-3596

Arkansas Division of Aging and Adult Services
Department of Social and Rehabilitative Services
Donaghey Building, Suite 1428
7th and Main Streets
Little Rock, AR 72201
501-371-2441

California Department of Aging
1600 K Street
Sacramento, CA 95814
916-322-5290

Colorado Aging and Adult Services Division
Department of Social Services
717 17th Street
P.O. Box 181000
Denver, CO 80218-0899
303-294-5913

Connecticut Department on Aging
175 Main Street
Hartford, CT 06106
203-566-3238

Delaware Division on Aging
Department of Health and Social Services
1901 North DuPont Highway
New Castle, DE 19720
302-421-6791

District of Colombia Office on Aging
1424 K Street, NW, 2nd Floor
Washington, DC 20011
202-724-5626

Florida Program Office of Aging
and Adult Services
Department of Health and
Rehabilitation Services
1317 Winewood Boulevard
Tallahassee, FL 32301
904-488-8922

Georgia Office of Aging
878 Peachtree Street, NE, Room
632
Atlanta, GA 30309
404-894-5333

Guam Public Health and Social
Services Department
Government of Guam
Agana, Guam 96910

Hawaii Executive Office on
Aging
Office of the Governor
335 Merchant Street, Room 241
Honolulu, HI 96813
808-548-2593

Idaho Office on Aging
Room 114, Statehouse
Boise, ID 83720
208-334-3833

Illinois Department on Aging
421 East Capitol Avenue
Springfield, IL 62701
217-785-2870

Indiana Department of Aging
and Community Services
251 North Illinois Street
P.O. Box 7083
Indianapolis, IN 46207
317-232-7006

Iowa Department of Elder Affairs
Suite 236, Jewett Building
914 Grand Avenue
Des Moines, IA 50319
515-281-5187

Kansas Department on Aging
610 West Tenth
Topeka, KS 66612
913-296-4986

Kentucky Division for Aging Services
Department of Human Resources
DHR Building — 6th Floor
275 East Main Street
Frankfort, KY 40601
502-564-6930

Louisiana Office of Elderly Affairs
P.O. Box 80374
Baton Rouge, LA 70898
504-925-1700

Maine Bureau of Elderly
Department of Human Services
State House — Station # 11
Augusta, ME 04333
207-289-2561

Maryland Office on Aging
State Office Building
301 West Preston Street, Room
   # 1004
Baltimore, MD 21201
301-225-1100

Massachusetts Executive Office
   of Elder Affairs
38 Chauncy Street
Boston, MA 02111
617-727-7750

Michigan Office of Services to
   the Aging
P.O. Box 30026
Lansing, MI 48909
517-373-8230

Minnesota Board on Aging
Metro Square Building — Room
   204
Seventh and Roberts Streets
St. Paul, MN 55101
612-296-2544

Mississippi Council on Aging
301 West Pearl Street
Jackson, MS 39203-3092
601-949-2070

Missouri Division on Aging
Department of Social Services
2701 West Main Street
Jefferson City, MO 65102
314-751-3082

Montana Community Services
   Division
P.O. box 4210
Helena, MT 59604
406-444-3865

Nebraska Department on Aging
P.O. Box 95044
301 Centennial Mall — South
Lincoln, NE 68509
402-471-2306

Nevada Division of Aging
Department of Human Resources
505 East King Street
Kinkead Building — Room 101
Carson City, NV 89710
702-885-4210

New Hampshire Council on
   Aging
105 Loudon Road — Building # 3
Concord, NH 03301
603-271-2751

New Jersey Division on Aging
Department of Community Affairs
P.O. Box 2768
363 West State Street
Trenton, NJ 08625
609-292-4833

New Mexico State Agency on
  Aging
224 East Palace Avenue, 4th
  Floor
La Villa Rivera Building
Santa Fe, NM 87501
505-827-7640

New York Office for the Aging
New York State Executive
  Department
Empire State Plaza
Agency Building No. 2
New York, NY 12223
518-474-5731

North Carolina Division on
  Aging
1985 Umpstead Drive — Kirby
  Building
Raleigh, NC 27603
919-733-3983

North Dakota Aging Services
Department of Human Services
State Capitol Building
Bismark, ND 58505
701-224-2577

Ohio Department on Aging
50 West Broad Street — 9th
  Floor
Columbus, OH 43215
614-466-5500

Oklahoma Special Unit on Aging
Department of Human Services
P.O. Box 25352
Oklahoma City, OK 73125
405-521-2281

Oregon Senior Services Division
313 Public Service Building
Salem, OR 97310
503-378-4728

Pacific Islands Trust Territory
Office of Elderly Programs
Community Development
  Division
Government of Trust Territory
  of the Pacific Islands
Saipan, Mariana Islands 96950

Pennsylvania Department of
  Aging
231 State Street
Harrisburg, PA 17101-1195
717-783-1550

Puerto Rico Gericulture Com-
  mission
Department of Social Services
P.O. Box 11398
Santurce, PR 00910
809-721-3141

Rhode Island Department of
  Elderly Affairs
79 Washington Street
Providence, RI 02903
401-277-2858

South Carolina Commission on
   Aging
400 Arbor Lake Drive, Suite B-
   500
Columbia, SC 29201
803-735-0210

South Dakota Office of Adult
   Services and Aging
700 North Illinois Street
Kneip Building
Pierre, SD 57501
605-773-3656

Tennessee Commission on Aging
706 Church Street, Suite 201
Nashville, TN 37219-5573
615-741-2056

Texas Department on Aging
P.O. Box 12786 Capitol Station,
   1949 IH 35
South Austin, TX 78741-3702]
512-444-2727

Utah Division of Aging and
   Adult Services
Department of Social Services
150 West North Temple
Box 45500
Salt Lake City, UT 84145-0500
801-533-6422

Vermont Office on Aging
103 South Main Street
Waterbury, VT 05676
802-241-2400

Virgin Islands Commission on
   Aging
6F Havensight Mall Charlotte
   Amalie
St. Thomas, VI 00801
809-774-5884

Virginia Department on Aging
101 North 14th Street — 18th
   Floor
James Monroe Building
Richmond, VA 23219
804-225-2271

Washington State Aging and
   Adult Services Administration
Department of Social and
   Health Services, OB-44A
Olympia, WA 98504
206-586-3786

West Virginia Commission on
   Aging
Holly Grove — State Capitol
Charleston, WV 25305
304-348-3317

Wisconsin Bureau of Aging
Division of Community Services
One West Wilson Street —
   Room 480
Madison, WI 53702
608-266-2536

Wyoming Commission on Aging
Hathaway Building — Room 139
Cheyenne, WY 82002-0710
307-777-7986

Private Organizations

American Association of Retired
  Persons
Health Advocacy Services
1909 K Street, NW
Washington, DC 20049
202-872-4700

American Bar Association
Commission on Legal Problems
  of the Elderly
1800 M Street, NW
Washington, DC 20036

American Health Care Association
1201 L Street, NW
Washington, DC 20005
202-833-2050

American Hospital Association
Division of Ambulatory Care
  and Health Promotion Services
840 North Lake Shore Drive
Chicago, IL 60611
312-280-6000

American Medical Association
535 North Dearborn Street
Chicago, IL 60610
(Write for organ donor cards)

Children of Aging Parents
2761 Trenton Road
Levittown, PA, 19056
215-945-6900

Cooperative Extension Service
(Your state university, or...)
University of New Hampshire
Durham, NH 03824
"Fact Sheets on Aging"

Family Service America
333 Seventh Avenue
New York, NY 10001
212-967-2740

Foundation for Hospice and
  Home Care
519 C Street, NE
Washington, DC 20002
202-547-6586

Gray Panthers
1424 16th Street, Suite 602
Washington, DC 20036

Health Insurance Association of
  America
1025 Connecticut Avenue, NW
Washington, DC 20036
202-223-7780

National Alliance for Senior
  Citizens
2525 Wilson Boulevard
Arlington, VA 22201

National Alzheimer's Association
70 E. Lake Street
Chicago, IL 60601-0379
312-853-3060 / 800-621-0379 /
  In Illinois: 800-572-6037
(with local chapters near you)

National Association of Area
  Agencies on Aging
600 Maryland Avenue, NW,
  Suite 208
Washington, DC 20024
202-484-7520
(Write for list of nearby agen-
  cies)

National Association of Meal
  Programs
204 E Street, NE
Washington, DC 20002
202-547-6157

National Association of Private
  Geriatric Care Managers
1315 Talbott Tower
Dayton, OH 45402
513-222-2621
(Write for list of nearby case
  managers)

National Council of Senior
  Citizens
925 15th Street, NW
Washington, DC 20005
202-347-8800

National Council on the Aging
600 Maryland Avenue, NW,
  West Wing 100
Washington, DC 20024
202-479-1200

National Foundation for Consumer Credit
8701 Georgia Avenue, Suite 601
Silver Spring, MD 20910

National Hispanic Council on
  Aging
2713 Ontario Road, NW
Washington, DC 20009
202-745-2521

National Hospice Organization
1901 North Moore Street, # 901
Arlington, VA 22209
703-243-5900

National League for Nursing
350 Hudson Street
New York, NY 10014
212-989-9393

Office of Scientific and Health
  Reports
National Institute of Neu-
  rological and Communicative
  Disorders and Stroke
National Institutes of Health
Building 31, Room 8A-06
Bethesda, MD 20892
301-496-5751
(publications list voluntary or-
  ganizations working in this
  subject area)

Older Women's League
730 11th Street, NW, Suite 300
Washington, DC 20001
202-783-6686

Public Citizen Health Research
  Group
2000 P Street, NW
Washington, DC 20036

SeniorNet Computer Network
399 Arguello Boulevard
San Francisco, CA 94118
415-750-5030

Society For The Right To Die
And Concern For Dying
New York, NY
212-246-6973

United Seniors Health Cooperative
1334 G Street, NW, Suite 500
Washington, DC 20005

... With an Emphasis on Hearing Problems

National Captioning Institute
5203 Leesburg Pike
Falls Church, VA 22041

Alexander Graham Bell Association For The Deaf
3417 Volta Place, NW
Washington, DC 20007

National Association of the Deaf
814 Thayer Avenue
Silver Spring, MD 20910
301-587-1788

AT&T National Special Needs
Center
2001 Route 46
Parsippany, NJ 07054

... With an Emphasis on Housing

American Association of Homes
For The Aging
1129 20th Street, NW, Suite 400
Washington, DC 20036
202-296-5960
(Write for list of homes nearby)

Design for Aging
American Institute of Architects
1735 New York Avenue, NW
Washington, DC 20007
202-626-7300
(Information on floor plans for
elderly)

National Citizens' Coalition on
Nursing Home Reform
1424 16th Street, NW
Washington, DC 20036
("Quality Care Advocate"
newsletter)

National Association for Home
Care
519 C Street, NE
Washington, DC 20002
202-547-7424

National Center for Home Equity Conversion
110 East Main, Room 1010
Madison, WI 53703

National Home Caring Council
235 Park Avenue South
New York, NY 10003

National Shared Housing
  Resource Center
6344 Greene Street
Philadelphia, PA 19144
215-848-1220

... With an Emphasis on Vision Problems

The Lighthouse
111 East 59th Street
New York, NY 10022

The Lions Club International
300 22nd Street
Oak Brook, IL 60570

National Society to Prevent
  Blindness
500 East Remington Road
Schaumburg, IL 60173

American Foundation for the
  Blind
15 West 16th Street
New York, NY 10011

Publications

Alzheimer's Disease: A Guide
  For Families
by Lenore S. Powell and Katie
  Courtice
Addison-Wesley Publishing Co,
  1983

Caregivers Guide: Help For Hel-
  pers Of The Aging (free)
Blue Cross/Blue Shield of Arizona
Corporate Communications
P.O. Box 13466
Phoenix, AZ 85002-3466

Home Care For The Elderly
by Jane Norris
McGraw Hill Books, 1987

The 36 Hour Day: A Family
  Guide To Caring For Persons
  With Alzheimer's Disease
by Nancy L. Mace and Peter V.
  Rabins
Johns Hopkins University Press,
  1982

The Illustrated Directory of
  Handicapped Products
Trio Publications
497 Cameron Way
Buffalo Grove, IL 60089

The Nursing Home Dilemma
by Doug Manning
Harper-Row, 1986

The Power of Attorney Book
Nolo Press
Berkeley, CA
800-992-6656 (CA: 800-640-6656)

Special Services

Mail Order Clothes and Accessories For The Disabled

E & J Avenues, Inc.: 800-848-
  2837
Sears Focus Health Care: 800-
  366-3000
Enrichments For Better Living:
  800-323-5547
Lumex Easy Living: 800-645-
  5272

Mail Order Discount Pharmacies

Price Club Pharmacy (Members
  Only): 800-726-2456
Medi-Mail: 800-331-1458

Low Cost Charge Cards

Bankcard Holders of America
560 Herndon Parkway, #120
Herndon, VA 22070
(Lists of low-rate, and no-fee
  charge cards)

Nursing Home Considerations

Your Personal Evaluation Checklist

For each nursing home you visit, consider whether each factor rates as inadequate, satisfactory, good, or exceptional:

Qualifications: How is the facility accredited? For how long? What are the credentials of management and staff? Is the home's manager or executive director available to you? What are the qualifications of the medical director? The head nurse? The nursing staff? Is the facility certified for Medicare? Medicaid?

Physical plant: Consider the number of rooms, the percent filled, and the number of people on the waiting list. Evaluate the overall quality, safety, and convenience of the location. Look carefully at the facility's overall cleanliness, brightness of lighting, and freshness of air, as well as its overall noise level, its provision of privacy for residents when needed, and the presence of working call buttons where needed. Is the bedroom spacious, comfortable, with storage areas for personal items? Does it have comfortable common areas, smoke-free areas, outdoor areas for relaxation or recreation? Are there adequate fire alarms, fire exits, and fire extinguishers? Are there safety rails in hallways and on the beds, non-skid flooring, protection (such as closed doors or handrails) against falls on steps? Look for wires, area rugs, and other obstructions on which residents can trip. Does the home provide enough wheelchairs and walkers for residents? How close is your parent's bathroom to the bed? Is there a library? A card room? A TV room? A music room? Is there a telephone on which your parent can call you whenever he or she wishes? What differences (if any) are there for private and for Medicaid residents?

Caregiving: Is the facility capable of providing intensive care? Skilled nursing care? Rehabilitation? Custodial care? Respite care? Are the residents generally clean, dressed for the day, and active? Do they move about the home or seem to stay in their rooms or common areas? What activities are scheduled? Can residents get their hair cut or styled? How often are they bathed? Are there volunteers working in the home? How promptly are call buttons answered? Who will take responsibility for day-to-day care of your parent? Who is responsible in an emergency? Can private physicians attend a patient regularly? How well are psychological factors considered along with physical factors in setting a resident's treatment plan?

Meals: What is a typical week's menu? How many meals per day? Can family members eat with your parent? How tasty, nutritious, and attractive are the meals? Are ingredients generally fresh, canned, or packaged? What is the overall cleanliness of the kitchen and kitchen staff? Will a resident's meals be specially prepared (sliced, diced, sauced, conformed to religious preferences, etc.) on request? Are portions large enough? How easily can your parent obtain a snack between meals, particularly between supper one day and breakfast the next? Will your parent generally eat in the bedroom, or in the dining room? Will aides help feed your parent as needed? Are uneaten meals rapidly cleaned up and taken away?

Activities: What special therapies are available to residents? Are physical and other therapists in the home licensed and registered? How useful is their equipment? How often are trips outside the home organized for the residents? Are stimulating lectures, courses, or other activities available? What is the role of the social worker in the home? Are provisions available for your parent to partake in his or her preferred religious observances? How often does the resident's council meet and work with those in authority? What sort of family-based volunteer and support activities are available?

Emotional Factors: What seem to be the staff attitudes toward residents? How do the staff interact with residents? How do residents interact with each other? How would you characterize the residents' apparent mood and level of contentment? The staff's overall feeling of supportiveness for residents?

Costs: What is the daily cost of the home? What extra costs are not included in this: medication, special treatments, canteen money, laundry, physician visits, other? What is the initial cost to place your parent in the facility? What is the likely monthly cost? How well are bills itemized? What is the procedure to redress errors in billing? When will any deposits be returned? How much do Medicaid residents receive in monthly spending money? Will your parent be able to stay once he or she has qualified for Medicaid?

Medicines To Watch

According to the U.S. Health Care Financing Administration, the following drugs (listed as generic name, followed by brand names) have often been inappropriately or excessively used to restrain patients in nursing homes.

Check your parent's medical chart and if one or more of these drugs is being administered, question the ordering physician and monitor carefully to make sure it is needed in the dosage ordered and that it is not producing any major side effects.

Acetophenazine (Tindal)
Chlorpromazine (Thorazine)
Chlorprothixene (Taractan)
Droperidol (Inapsine)
Fluphenazine (Prolixin, Permitil)
Fluphenazine Decanoate
   (Prolixin Decanoate)
Haloperidol (Haldol)
Haloperidol Decanoate (Haldol
   Decanoate)
Loxapine (Loxitane)
Mesoridazine (Serentil)
Molindone (Moban)
Perphenazine (Trilafon)
Pimozide (Orap)
Promazine (Sparine)
Thioridazine (Mellaril)
Thiothixene (Navane)
Trifluoperazine (Stelazine)
Triflupromazine (Vesprin)

Updates to This Resource Guide:

For a free updated and expanded copy of this resource guide, send a stamped, self-addressed envelope to:

Resource Guide Update
Key Publications
P.O. Box 6375
Woodland Hills, CA 91365

To order a copy of this complete book, send $19.95 plus $3.50 (shipping and handling) to the address above, or charge the book to Visa or MasterCard by calling the Key Publications Order Line:
800-735-0015

Glossary

Acute care: Health care services provided for a person with a disease, injury, or other ailment requiring immediate attention.

Adaptive devices: Special hardware, clothing, and tools that help a disabled person compensate for disability and perform various chores and activities more independently.

Aging Syndrome: The pattern of physical, emotional, functional, and social changes that are often associated with advanced age.

Aides or Attendants: People trained in basic care procedures who provide help as needed with eating, bathing, bladder and bowel functions and household chores.

Alzheimer's Disease: A degenerative disease of the brain that leads to mental confusion, inability to perform daily tasks, emotional changes and mood swings, and ultimately death.

Artificial Nourishment: A medical procedure by which a person who is unable to eat ordinary foods can be fed through tubes entering the body. Because the tubes are uncomfortable, the person must usually be tied down and/or sedated.

Asset Transfer: A legal procedure by which stocks, bonds, artwork, a home, or other valuable property is deeded to an organization or individual in return for some benefit, usually free use of the asset for the remainder of the donor's life, or lifetime room, board, and care.

Assisted Living Facility: One of several different types of living quarters where a disabled person is helped by aides to cope with ordinary chores, routines, and responsibilities. Provides less care than a nursing home.

Bath Lift: A device that assists a disabled person to enter and exit a bath or shower.

Board-and-Care homes: State-licensed living facilities in private homes, apartments, or hotels for elderly people. They do not provide as much care as nursing homes and usually require some degree of physical independence.

Case Manager: Advisor and helper who can evaluate and arrange appropriate care for a wide range of medical and emotional conditions. Private case managers charge for their time, and provide their services either during an initial period, or to monitor a patient over a very long time.

Co-insurance: (Co-payment) A cost-sharing system that requires the patient to pay out of pocket for part of the cost of his or her care.

Congregate Housing: A living arrangement in which unrelated people share a dwelling cooperatively in order to assist each other in maintaining a viable household.

Continuing Care Community: An organized arrangement of dwellings and services designed to provide varying degrees of assistance, support, and medical care for elderly people as they progress from independent living to greater degrees of dependence on others. Often includes the range from self-supporting apartments and homes to full-service nursing care facilities. Residents are fully independent when they move in, then gradually shift to more supportive settings within the community, as needed.

Dementia: Not a disease, but a group of symptoms resulting from disease and deterioration, characterized by intellectual decline that impairs even routine functioning.

Drop Attack: A sudden fall experienced for any reason. It may result in significant injury and anxiety.

Durable Power of Attorney: An important document a person can execute which authorizes another to control the person's legal and other affairs when the person becomes unable to do so.

Elder Cottage: A portable dwelling unit intended for older people, and normally placed relatively near the home of their caregivers, such as their adult children.

Elder Law: The specific laws dealing with the rights of the elderly and the power of other individuals and the state to control and interfere in their affairs.

Extended Care Facility: A nursing home or other institution designed and operated to provide long-term care for patients who most often are not likely to regain their health.

Functional Assessment: A medical and psychological evaluation of an individual to see how well they can cope with everyday chores, routines, and responsibilities, and to identify the causes of any problems and seek remedies or other means of improvement.

Generational Differences: The variances in values, perceptions, skills, attitudes, and ability to cope between people of significantly different ages.

Geriatrics: The branch of medicine dealing with the special disorders and conditions associated with aging.

Guardian: Person appointed by the court to handle the affairs of another person deemed incompetent or incapable of managing his or her own decisions and finances.

Health Care Power of Attorney: An important document a person can execute which authorizes another to control the person's medical care when the person becomes unable to do so.

HMO: Health Maintenance Organization, provides medical services at a limited number of hospitals and doctors' offices for a fixed monthly fee and (sometimes) a co-payment. May provide an alternative to Medicare and medigap insurance coverage.

Home Health Agency: A public or private organization that makes available skilled nurses and other therapists to provide services in a patient's home.

Home Health Aide: Trained medical assistants who work under the supervision or a nurse or physician, and who provide personal care services. They administer medication, change bandages, monitor vital signs and perform daily living support services like feeding, bathing, and grocery shopping.

Home Visiting Services: Organizations and agencies that provide health, social, or other needed services directly to individuals in their homes.

Homemaker: Specially trained individuals who regularly provide household cleaning, cooking, grocery shopping, laundry, and other such services in the home of a person who cannot do these chores alone.

Hospice: A unique form of medical and social service care for terminally ill patients that emphasizes pain control, symptom management, and emotional support rather than life-sustaining technology.

Identity Bracelet: A wristband or other device carrying name, address, telephone, and other information about the wearer, intended to convey this information to others in the event the wearer cannot.

Incontinence: Inability to control bladder or bowel functions, often associated with old age, which can result from any of a large number of underlying causes, many of which can be improved by treatment.

Intermediate Care Facility: A halfway house between hospital and home, sometimes located in a nursing home or extended care facility, where individuals can receive medical care and therapeutic treatment at lower cost, and for a longer time, than is possible in a hospital setting.

Invasive Procedures: Medical treatment that involves penetrating some part of the body or otherwise interfering with bodily processes.

Involuntary Financial Management: A condition in which the court appoints a guardian or other financial manager to control the assets and income of an individual who is judged unable to do so alone.

Life Care Community: See "Continuing Care Community."

Living Will: A legal document intended to record and convey the wishes of the individual regarding medical treatment for a life-threatening illness or injury. The living will is not binding on medical professionals.

Meals on Wheels: Private programs sponsored by charitable and religious organizations to regularly deliver fully prepared, well-balanced meals to house-bound individuals at low- or no-cost.

Medicaid: Federal and state programs of health insurance for people 65 and older, as well as disabled and low income families. This program covers costs of long-term care for the indigent, but as many as forty percent of those who should be eligible do not apply for Medicaid.

Medicare: Federal program of health insurance for people 65 and older, and some disabled Americans. This program does not cover the cost of long-term care.

Medicare Assignment: A process by which a doctor or other provider of medical care agrees to accept Medicare's payment schedule as payment in full, except for specific co-insurance and deductible amounts the patient must pay.

Medigap Insurance: Any of a wide variety of private policies intended to cover medical costs not fully covered or paid by Medicare.

Nursing home: A skilled nursing facility providing a full range of board, care, and medical services to those recovering from hospitalization and those unable to live at home.

Occupational Therapist: Assists patients in developing or regaining capabilities as part of their rehabilitation. Also recommends adaptive devices to assist them in more independent living.

Ombudsman: Independent nursing home investigator responsible for monitoring the care of certain facilities, reporting violations to appropriate authorities, and intervening with nursing home management as requested by residents and their caregivers.

Para-transit: A community sponsored transportation program designed to assist disabled people in getting to and from grocery shopping, medical appointments, and other activities. The cost for a ride, which must usually be scheduled a day or more in advance, is normally very low. Many vans are equipped to carry wheelchairs.

Personal Emergency Response System: A device installed in a person's home which can be triggered, sometimes by remote control, to call for medical or other help when the person is unable to do so manually.

Physical Therapist: Specialist who helps patients regain or attain physical capabilities after illness or physical injury.

Power of Attorney: An important document a person can execute which authorizes another to control the person's affairs. See "Durable Power of Attorney" and "Health Care Power of Attorney."

Primary Care Physician: The doctor a person most commonly calls first when a problem arises, and who refers the individual to specialists as needed. In an HMO, this is the "gatekeeper" who must be seen first, and who must authorize all (reimbursed) visits to other doctors and medical providers.

Provider: Person or institution (public or private) that offers a service related to health care. Usually a doctor, therapist, or hospital.

Quality of Life: The overall feeling of enjoyment, satisfaction, personal happiness, independence, and freedom a person experiences in the normal course of living. The more intense these feelings are, the higher the "quality of life" is said to be.

Representative Payee: A person legally designated to receive Social Security benefits intended for another, and charged with using the money for the original beneficiary.

Residential Care Facility: An assisted living facility.

Respite Care: A service for regular caregivers (mainly of children and the disabled) that provides them with short-term relief from ongoing responsibilities.

Retirement Community: Living units integrated with recreational and social facilities to create a nearly self-contained neighborhood or small town where older people can find companionship, security, and stimulation.

Retirement Hotel: A residence facility offering bedrooms or small suites (usually without cooking facilities), and providing regular meals, linen service, and occasionally other services geared to the needs of the elderly residents.

Retirement Planning: A special form of financial planning that considers the long-term impact of income, expense, and inflation factors, and aims to provide adequate financial resources for the expected remaining lifetime of the individual.

Sandwich Generation: A popular phrase for those born in the 1940s and 1950s who are "sandwiched" between caregiving responsibilities for their children and for their aging parents.

Senility: Also called *dementia*. Once considered a normal part of aging, now doctors view this as the result of disease and deterioration.

Senior Adult Day Center: Facility providing a supportive atmosphere, supervision, stimulation, recreation and sometimes treatment and rehabilitation for aging adults who live at home and visit the center during specific hours of operation.

Shared Housing: Congregate housing.

Sheltered Housing: A protected housing situation usually intended for those with mental, but not necessarily physical, deficits.

Social Worker: Trained professional who deals with the social and emotional needs of the elderly and their families. Some of the best case managers began as social workers.

Support Groups: Informal meetings attended by people with similar responsibilities and problems, in which attendees offer their own experience and support to help themselves and others feel better and endure longer.

Supplemental Insurance: Optional policies purchased to provide reimbursement for health care expenses not fully covered by Medicare.

Telephone Reassurance: A program in which ill, frail, or house-bound individuals are called regularly to verify that they are safe and sound, and to provide them briefly with reassurance and personal contact.

Treatment Plan: An organized approach to remedy a disorder, ideally arrived at through consultations with various professionals in a group discussion process.

Visiting Nurse: Trained professional nurse who visits a patient in the home to monitor vital signs and physical condition and execute a physician's treatment orders.

Voluntary Financial Management: A situation in which one person executes the needed documents to allow another to help manage his or her assets and income.

Volunteer Ombudsman: See "Ombudsman."

Index

About The Authors

Francine Moskowitz is president of Alpha Consulting Associates, Los Angeles, California. Her clients include hospitals, health systems, physicians and physician groups. Prior to founding Alpha Consulting Associates in 1984, she was instrumental in opening low-cost housing for seniors in California, and in developing an innovative, nation-wide network of hospitals across the country serving the special needs of senior citizens. Ms. Moskowitz has been Chief Operating Officer of a network of diagnostic imaging centers, Vice President — marketing and strategic planning, for a major public company providing ambulatory care, and Director of Program Development for a large, diversified health-care company. In the 1970s, she served as Director of Program Development and Special Projects for an East Coast medical center. She holds a Master's Degree from Hahnemann Medical College and a Bachelor's Degree from Temple University.

Robert Moskowitz is a business consultant who writes frequently on strategic management, productivity, and office automation. In addition to being an award-winning industrial filmmaker, he is the producer of ten educational and training programs on various business, management, and investment topics published by leading management education services, and the author of *How To Organize Your Work and Your Life*, originally published by Doubleday in 1981 and now in its third printing. Mr. Moskowitz's professional background includes more than twenty-two years of consulting, writing, and media productions in such areas as business management, finance, and investment. He is presently at work on his first novel. He holds a Bachelor's Degree from the University of Pennsylvania.